Raymond E. Brown, S.S.

With my best wishes
Raymond E. Brown

A Risen Christ in Eastertime

Essays on the Gospel Narratives
of the Resurrection

The Liturgical Press
Collegeville, Minnesota

Three of the essays reprinted here were originally published in *Worship* (under the usual rules of ecclesiastical approbation) as follows:

"The Resurrection in Matthew (27:62–28:20) March 1990, 157–170
"The Resurrection in John 20 . . . ," May 1990, 194–206
"The Resurrection in John 21 . . . ," September 1990, 433–445

Cover design by Mary Jo Pauly

Nihil obstat: Robert C. Harren, *Censor deputatus.*
Imprimatur: ✝ Jerome Hanus, O.S.B., October 26, 1990.

1   2   3   4   5   6   7   8   9

Library of Congress Cataloging-in-Publication Data

Brown, Raymond Edward.
    A risen Christ in Eastertime : essays on the Gospel narratives of the Resurrection / Raymond E. Brown.
      p. cm.
    ISBN 0-8146-2014-0
    1. Jesus Christ—Resurrection—Biblical teaching. 2. Bible. N.T. Gospels—Criticism, interpretation, etc. I. Title.
    BT481.B76 1990   90-22728
    226'.06—dc20   CIP

Contents

Foreword

Comparable in scope and format to this book, The Liturgical Press has published three volumes of my biblical reflections on the Gospel passages used by the Church respectively in the liturgies of Advent (Matthew 1 and Luke 1), Christmas (Matthew 2 and Luke 2), and Holy Week (the four Passion Narratives). As I turn now to the Gospel passages of Eastertime, my goal remains the same: to make the rich insights of modern biblical exegesis conveniently available for reflection during the great feasts of the liturgical year.

Elsewhere I have written on the resurrection from the viewpoint of historical criticism.[1] There I commented on the earliest preaching references to the raising of Jesus (e.g., Acts 5:30) and to his appearances (1 Cor 15:5-8); I investigated whether a bodily resurrection and an empty tomb were presumed from the beginning, even if narratives of the empty tomb were late; and I endeavored to reconcile the sharp divergences in those narratives. With none of that am I concerned in this volume, for now my interest is *to see how the treatment of the resurrection in an individual Gospel fits the theology and plan of that Gospel.*

Modern biblical scholarship insists that each Gospel has its own integrity and distinct outlook; and overall the liturgical lectionary has been guided by this principle since it reads consistently through one Gospel on the Ordinary Sundays of the Year (Matthew in Year I; Mark in Year II; Luke in Year III), rather than indiscriminately mixing passages from different Gospels as in times past. In Eastertime itself, however, the lectionary departs from the consecutive Gospel approach.

---

[1] *The Virginal Conception and Bodily Resurrection* (New York: Paulist, 1973). More recently and concisely, see my article in *The New Jerome Biblical Commentary* (Englewood Cliffs: Prentice Hall, 1990) 81:118-134.

On Holy Saturday and Easter Sunday various Gospels supply the pericopes; on the Second Sunday of Easter in all three years the passages are from John; and on the weekdays of the Easter octave pericopes from the different Gospels are gone through with the interest that every tomb or appearance account in the New Testament be read.

While one can understand the joyous desire to hear as much as possible about the resurrection of Jesus, the deeper understanding of the Gospel narratives, which is related to the individual evangelist's overall view of Jesus, suffers. By concentrating on that aspect in these essays, perhaps I can enhance the appreciation of the resurrection on the part of those who reflect on the lectionary, since in a given year an individual Gospel will have been read on Sundays, and the respective resurrection passage from that Gospel will evoke memories of those readings.

In this volume I shall cover all the Gospel passages dealing with the resurrection, i.e., accounts both of the visits to the empty tomb and of the appearances of Jesus. In each chapter I shall explain any peculiarities about what I have included, e.g., the addition to Mark constituted by 16:9-20, or the complement to the Gospel of Luke offered by Acts 1:1-12. Only in John does the resurrection account cover two chapters, and I shall devote an essay to each.

Even though each Gospel has its own emphasis in narrating the raising of Jesus, when readers move from one Gospel to the other, a fascinating picture emerges. There is in the accounts a whole spectrum of reactions, ranging from hostility through puzzlement to spontaneous faith, so that the resurrection functions as a final test of response to Jesus. In commenting on the passion I became convinced that the Gospel narratives were meant to pose to the readers the question: "What stance would you have taken were you there when this happened?" As I wrote this book, I became aware of a similar goal of the evangelists: "In the days surrounding the

Foreword

first Easter which of the reactions recounted would have been yours?'' The fact that those who feature in the stories often doubted or misunderstood is a warning that the answer to the question requires meditation. This volume will serve well if it prompts such meditation.

I dedicate it with sincere gratitude to Eileen Tobin, undauntedly vital through years three score and fifteen, many of them difficult. This is a small and inadequate tribute for the great service she rendered me in nine years as my secretary at Union Theological Seminary in New York City. Remembering her distinct preference for typing manuscripts over correspondence (although she was far better than I at the latter when I gave her free hand), I pray that she will have many years and good health, so that in retirement she can at last have the leisure to exercise her own writing skills in which she takes much pleasure. She will then enrich other lives as she has already enriched mine.

Foreword

Chapter 1

The Resurrection in Mark (16:1-8; 16:9-20)

In some ways Mark remains the most difficult Gospel. Although in seminary courses it may well be the most frequently taught, it is surely the least familiar of the four Gospels to many Christians, especially to Catholics. It was scarcely ever read on Sunday in the pre-Vatican II lectionary; and in citations of passages shared by the Synoptic Gospels, Matthew, functioning as "the Church's Gospel," was quoted by preference.[2] Even among scholars who have studied Mark with great intensity, it remains a conundrum, producing little or no consensus as to sources, locale, or goals. The terse Marcan style, which leaves much unexplained, has been an open invitation for imaginative theorizing.[3]

Mark 16, the chapter pertinent to the resurrection, is a prime example of how since the second century Mark has confounded attempts at understanding. Only the first eight verses of the chapter are safely attested as having belonged to the original Gospel. Yet 16:8, which follows an authoritative angelic instruction to speak of the import of the resurrection to the disciples and Peter, has the women who were so instructed "say nothing to anyone for they were afraid." With great difficulty scholars have come up with a grammatical parallel for the abrupt phrasing of this ending, but that parallel does not solve the issue of how what is related in

[2]The fact that before 1960 Catholics were officially taught that Matthew either directly or indirectly (in translation) was written by an eyewitness member of the Twelve was also a factor.

[3]The range of views is illustrated by the thesis of a few, but important, scholars that canonical Mark is a censored, bowdlerized version of an esoteric gospel of less sober caliber, as seen in the *Secret Gospel of Mark*, mentioned in a letter of Clement of Alexandria. H. Koester who holds this view dates canonical Mark to around 180!

16:8 constitutes a suitable conclusion to what began in 1:1 as "The Good News of Jesus Christ." How is it good news that the women were afraid to tell anyone of Jesus' resurrection? Textual witnesses of Mark that do not terminate with 16:8 offer three variant continuations, only one of which has enough frequency to be considered traditional. That one, known as the "Long Ending," is Mark 16:9-20, which appears in all Catholic and most Protestant Bibles (sometimes in the latter in smaller print or as a footnote in order to indicate textual doubt).

Since liturgically Mark 16:1-8 and the most widely attested ending (16:9-20) tend to be read as separate pericopes,[4] I think it best in this series to treat 16:1-8 as if Mark intended to end the Gospel there.[5] Following the treatment of 16:1-8, I shall ask how 16:9-20 makes sense as part of the canonical text of Mark.[6]

MARK 16:1-8: THE WOMEN AT THE TOMB

The principal characters in this scene are the women: Mary Magdalene, Mary of James, and Salome. We were introduced to these three in 15:40-41 (where the second Mary was designated as "of James the less [younger] and of Joses"). There they were identified as women who had followed Jesus when he was in Galilee and ministered to him, and who were now

[4]In the B year Mark 16:1-8 is the selection for the Easter Vigil and (as alternative) for the morning Easter Mass. Mark 16:9-15 is read on Saturday in Easter week, and 16:15-20 on Ascension Thursday in the B year.

[5]The Marcan situation which involves manuscript evidence differs from that of John. There it is purely a scholarly hypothesis to treat John 20 as the end of the Gospel, for there is no ancient manuscript that lacks John 21.

[6]The Council of Trent insisted on its list of books "as sacred and canonical in their entirety *with all their parts* according to the text usually read in the Catholic Church and as they are in the ancient Latin Vulgate." Discussions clarified that Mark 16:9-20 was included among the "parts." Yet that Tridentine statement about canonicity does not settle the issue of whether Mark wrote 16:9-20.

The Resurrection in Mark

at a distance observing the death of Jesus on the cross. In so describing them, Mark kept them clearly distinct from "his disciples" and/or "the Twelve" who were companions of Jesus at the Last Supper (14:12, 17), who went with him to Gethsemane on the Mount of Olives (14:26, 32), and all of whom fled when he was arrested (14:50). What would Mark have us think of these women?[7] Mark insists that Jesus died alone, abandoned by all his disciples. While these women were not among the disciples who abandoned him, their presence distant from the cross could have been of no consolation to him. The women had not been put through the same test as the disciples who were physically closer to him in Gethsemane and failed. Are the women positive models to the Christian readers? Or are they those who once followed him in Galilee but are now passive onlookers? Or have they not failed simply because they have not been tested?

The second Marcan reference to them during the passion (15:47) does not answer these questions. Joseph of Arimathea, "who was himself looking for the kingdom of God," whether or not he was a disciple,[8] did a pious act by getting permission from Pilate to take Jesus' body and bury it. Mark tells us that "Mary Magdalene and Mary of Joses saw where Jesus was laid." Why they did not participate in Joseph's burial of Jesus is never explained and so the impression of uninvolved onlookers persists.

To an extent the ambiguity about the women is partially resolved in the scene we are discussing when Mark reports that after the Sabbath was past (thus sometime after approxi-

---

[7]While without doubt the two groups are kept distinct in the passion narrative, scholars dispute whether in Mark "disciples" ever includes such women followers. In Matthew the term does not, but Mark is less clear.

[8]In *CBQ* 50 (1988) 233-245 I argued that in Mark's understanding this member of the Sanhedrin was not a disciple at the time of Jesus' death (even if he may have become one later)—that may explain why the women could not join Joseph in the burial.

The Resurrection in Mark

mately 6:00 P.M. on Saturday) the women at last get involved on Jesus' behalf, for they buy spices in order to go and anoint him.[9] In Mark 14:8 Jesus revealed that the anointing of his body by an unnamed woman had been a preparation for his forthcoming burial. This plan of the three women to anoint Jesus after burial will be the occasion for revealing his resurrection.

Mark gives a second time-reference which fixes the moment when the women acted on their intention; it was "very early on the first day of the week." Throughout the Marcan passion narrative there has been an extraordinary sequence of precise three-hour time intervals: the story began with "evening" on the first day of the unleavened bread when Jesus ate the supper with his disciples (14:12, 17); it continued through cockcrow when Peter concluded his denials (14:72) and a morning hour when Jesus was given over to Pilate (15:1); and it culminated with the third, sixth, and ninth hours as he hung on the cross (15:25, 33; i.e., 9:00 A.M., noon, 3:00 P.M.); only at "evening" was Jesus at last buried (15:42).

Not without plausibility scholars have suggested that such time precisions mean that already within Mark's experience there were set times of commemorative prayers as Christians recalled the death of the Lord. The references in 16:1-2 to the end of the Sabbath and to the early hour on the first day of the week may be part of the same picture.[10] The further

[9]There is considerable scholarly discussion as to whether the intent to anoint a corpse several days after burial is historically plausible. I wish to express the caution that Mark would have wanted his account to be plausible about such an incidental. He is a better guide to plausibility in burial practices of the first century than are 20th-century scholars who base their judgments on the very limited available knowledge about burial in that period.

[10]There are psalm references to morning (early, hour of wakening) as a time of prayer and of awareness of God (17:15; 30:6; 59:17; 101:8). Mark's descriptions of the day of burial as the day before the Sabbath (15:42), of the Sabbath as being past (16:1), and of the first day of the week (16:2) fulfill Jesus' predictions of resurrection "after three days" (8:31; 9:31; 10:34). Yet it

The Resurrection in Mark

specification that "the sun had risen" may be a symbolic reference to the resurrection having already taken place. Mark 8:22-26 shows a symbolic interest in seeing and blindness, and that at least makes possible a symbolic interest in light and darkness.

In 16:3-4 the women pose a rhetorical question to themselves as to who will roll away the stone that has been placed at the door of the tomb, and we are reminded that this was a very large stone. The picture helps to reinforce the contrast between human incapacity and God's power. When Mark reports that the women saw the stone already rolled back, he is using the passive to indicate divine action. God has undone the sealing that the Sanhedrin member Joseph of Arimathea so carefully placed (15:46).

As the women look inside the tomb, they see a young man sitting on the right side (a place of dignity) clothed with a white robe. He is surely a divine spokesman;[11] and the amazement that greets him is typical of the reaction to the appearance of angels. In addition, however, this reaction at the end of the Marcan Gospel constitutes an inclusion with the amazement that greeted Jesus when he drove out an evil spirit at the beginning of the Gospel (1:25-27). There the demon addressed him as "Jesus the Nazarene" (1:24), and so it is not surprising in the present scene to hear the heavenly appearance in the tomb tell the women that he knows that they are seeking "Jesus the Nazarene." This makes the reader certain that the same person who at the beginning of

is significant that the tomb stories do not refer to "the third day" but to "the first day of the week." How early, without abandoning their reverence for the Sabbath, did Jewish Christians begin to give reverence to the next day, the first of the week, because it was associated with the Lord's resurrection?

[11]Despite the imaginative attempts of some scholars to identify him with the young man who fled away naked from Gethsemane (14:51-52), Matt 28:2 and Luke 24:23 were correct in understanding Mark to refer to an angelic appearance (also John 20:12).

The Resurrection in Mark

the Gospel manifested his power over evil is the one in whom God now manifests His power over death. From beginning to end Satan has been defeated by Jesus the Nazarene.

From the initial act of Jesus' power and throughout his ministry, those attracted to him could not fully recognize or believe in his divine identity because he had not yet suffered on the cross (8:31-33; 9:31-32). Now at last the angelic youth can add the crucial identification of Jesus the Nazarene, namely, "the one who was crucified." It is only of Jesus the Nazarene who has died on the cross that the triumphal affirmation "He has been raised" (16:6) makes sense in God's plan. The women have been inside the tomb looking about. Yet it is not tautological that having said, "He has been raised," the heavenly youth goes on to say: "He is not here; see the place where they laid him."[12] The significance of the empty tomb in terms of the resurrection of the one who was crucified is not a matter of simple observation. Because of the youth's message the women now know that their well-meaning search for Jesus was in vain.

The Marcan scene, however, is more than a revelation of the resurrection, for 16:7 reports a commission given to the women by the heavenly youth—a commission that makes clear that the risen, crucified Jesus of Nazareth has still more to do. At the beginning of the passion Jesus predicted the loss of faith (*skandalizein*) and scattering of all his disciples who had come with him to the Last Supper. This prediction was not without a ray of hope, however: "But after I am raised up, I will go before you to Galilee" (14:28). The angelic youth hearkens back to that promise: "Go tell his disciples and Peter that he is going before you to Galilee; there you

---

[12]Gen 5:24 reports that Enoch was not found because God had translated him (to the other world), but we are not told that Enoch had died. There is no silence about Jesus' death.

The Resurrection in Mark

will see him as he told you" (16:7).[13] The disciples may have utterly failed even to the point where one would-be follower fled away naked (14:52) and Peter cursed Jesus, swearing that he did not even know this man (14:71). Yet Mark indicates that this failure can be overcome if the disciples go back to Galilee where Jesus called them at the beginning of the story (1:14-20—still another inclusion).[14] Thus the Marcan readers are not left in total suspense about the fate of Jesus' disciples: he has no intention of losing them permanently. In 10:32 Jesus went before his disciples on the road to Jerusalem while warning them that there the Son of Man would be given over, condemned to death, killed, and after three days be raised up. All his words have proved true, and now he will go before them back to Galilee and there reunite them. Those who were "scattered" (14:27) by the events of the passion at Jerusalem will once more become a community when they return to the place where they were first called together as disciples. This will happen because God will make them see Jesus the Nazarene raised from the dead, the victor over crucifixion whom they had committed themselves to follow.

If the angelic message in 16:7 concerns the disciples and Peter, Mark's primary attention is still centered on the women who had been given this angelic revelation. Their

[13]In 16:5-7 Mark supplies a double inclusion, one inclusion with the beginning of the whole Gospel (1:24-27) and one with the beginning of the passion (14:27-28).

[14]Nothing in Mark suggests that this geographical direction is meant to support Galilean Christianity over Jerusalem Christianity. (After all, in the early years of postresurrectional Christianity Peter, mentioned specifically here, was associated with Jerusalem Christianity and no longer with Galilee.) Nor is there much to support the thesis that Mark related Galilee to the Gentile mission as Matt 4:15 does. The specific mention of Peter who failed outstandingly in the passion shows that "Galilee" is meant to reverse the fate of the disciples during the passion. I do not exclude the added possibility that Mark's use of the place name is meant to remind the reader of all that Jesus taught and said there in the presence of this disciples.

The Resurrection in Mark

reaction (16:8) has to be a total surprise to the readers. Instead of going forth to the disciples to proclaim with joy that Jesus had been raised and has positive plans for them in Galilee, the women flee from the tomb overcome with trembling, amazement, and fear. They tell nothing to anyone. Inevitably scholars have speculated about the reasons for the silence, at times offering suggestions that have little to do with Mark's expressed line of thought;[15] yet there is where the answer lies. Throughout the Gospel Mark has shown how those who followed Jesus failed because they did not understand that Jesus had to suffer or because they were unwilling to accompany him into his passion. Because of the when, where, and how of the appearance of these three women in the passion story (after the death, watching from a distance), readers would get the impression that they had excaped the great trial. Above I have described their coming to the tomb to anoint Jesus as their first act of involvement in the passion. Here, although they have received the revelation of the risen Lord and an angelic commission to proclaim him, they fail. The final words with which Mark describes their failure are: "For they were afraid." This uncomplimentary portrait is in harmony with Mark's somber insistence that none can escape suffering in the following of Jesus.

Amidst Mark's readers surely there were some who had been tested by persecution and had failed. They could find encouragement in the story of Jesus' own disciples, all of whom failed during the passion. But others among Mark's readers would not have been so tested. There is a parallel between them and the women who appear on the scene only after the crucifixion and observe his death without having become involved even in his burial. Like the women they are

---

[15]Surely Mark is not interested in explaining why the empty tomb story has appeared so late in Christian tradition or in suppressing the memory of a resurrection appearance to the women because they could not serve as legal witnesses.

The Resurrection in Mark

will-inclined, but after they hear the proclamation of the resurrection and receive an commission to proclaim what has happened to Jesus, they too can fail if they become afraid. Mark's enduring warning, then, would be that not even the resurrection guarantees true faith in Jesus' followers, for the resurrection cannot be appropriated unless one has been tried. People may say that they believe firmly in the risen Christ, but they must realize existentially in their own lives that the one they are following is none other than Jesus the Nazarene who was *crucified.* Mark who has been somber in describing discipleship throughout the passion remains somber about the requirements of discipleship after the resurrection.

MARK 16:9-20 (THE "LONG ENDING"):
THREE APPEARANCES OF JESUS

That grammatically this addition is awkwardly attached to Mark 16:1-8 is obvious from the way 16:9 begins: "Now, having risen early on the first day of the week, he appeared first to Mary Magdalene from whom he had thrown out seven demons." Although the "early on the first day of the week" *partially* echoes Mark 16:1,[16] the readers are introduced to Magdalene as if she had not hitherto been encountered as one of the main protagonists in the preceding verses. Moreover, the readers are not introduced to the unnamed "he"; the Jesus who is meant was not an active subject previously in 16:1-8, for there the "he" was the heavenly young man who interpreted the empty tomb.

More important than grammatical awkwardness in the joining is the theological suitability of an appearance to Magdalene. Mark 16:8 left her fleeing in fear and trembling,

---

[16]"Partially" because the wording for "first" is different, and because the chronological indication in Mark 16:1 refers to the time of the visit to the empty tomb, while here the reference is to a time *before* that, when Jesus had risen.

The Resurrection in Mark

disobediently silent, failing to communicate the angel's directive to the disciples. Whoever added 16:9 had to assume that Mark did not deny hope to Magdalene despite her behavior.[17] In that assumption he was surely correct: if Mark could report a promised appearance in Galilee to disciples who had fled abandoning the Lord himself when he was arrested, and to a Peter who had denied and cursed the Lord, he could not have been less optimistic about Jesus' mercy to a woman who had failed to obey an angel. Indeed, the way Magdalene is identified makes sense precisely on that score. Jesus had already delivered her from demons (see Luke 8:2); he would scarcely abandon her now.

This appearance of Jesus to Magdalene[18]—literally, his becoming visible—gives her the courage to do the very thing that the angel had previously commanded: she goes to tell "those who had been with him" (the Twelve [Eleven]; Mark 3:14; 16:14), who were mourning and weeping. In describing the reaction of these disciples to Magdalene's message, the author of the Long Ending shows that he shares the pessimistic view of Jesus' followers that characterizes Mark. He reports (16:11) that when these disciples heard that Jesus was alive and had been seen by Magdalene, they were unbelieving.

Disbelief does not defeat the risen Lord, for afterwards he appears "in another form" to two *of them* as they are going

[17]The issue of relating Mark 16:1-8 and the Long Ending is important, for readers of copies of Mark would scarcely be expected to know that two different hands had composed 16:1-8 and 16:9-20 when they were sequential on the same page.

[18]Matt 28:9-10 and John 20:14 narrate an appearance to Magdalene although the wording of those accounts is not the same as the Long Ending's. I do not plan to debate here the relationship of the Long Ending to the other Gospels. Did its composer have a copy of all or some of the other Gospels before him; or did he sometimes draw on memories of the other Gospels that he had read or heard previously; or did he draw independently on traditions similar to those that had been employed in the other Gospels?

The Resurrection in Mark

into the countryside.[19] The reference to "another form" tells us how Christians came to explain why Jesus could not be easily recognized. Evidently, however, such a different appearance is enough to overcome previous disbelief, for the two return (to the city of Jerusalem) to tell the rest of the disciples. Just as they had not believed Magdalene, the others do not believe these two. Thus the Long Ending presents us with a remarkable sequence where only an encounter with the risen Jesus himself overcomes previous failure to believe. The harshness of Jesus' rebuke to "the rest" of the disciples (who clearly include the Eleven) for their disbelief and hardness of heart (16:14) is intelligible in light of the reason offered: "They had not believed those who had seen him (after he had been) raised." The community that is reading or hearing Mark consists of people who have to believe those who saw the risen Jesus, and the Long Ending is insisting that such faith was demanded by Jesus even of "those whom he also named apostles" (Mark 3:14 [variant reading]).

When Jesus makes himself visible to the Eleven, they are at table. In other Gospels the appearance of the risen Lord at meals has a eucharistic import,[20] but Mark 16:14 does nothing to emphasize that. If the eucharistic connection was known to the readers of the Long Ending, the rebuke by Jesus about obduracy and disbelief could have been seen as a comment on the failure of those who took part in the eucharistic meal to discern the presence of Jesus (somewhat as in 1 Cor 11:20-34, especially 11:29).

Be that as it may, the primacy in the Long Ending's account of this third appearance of Jesus centers on another feature characteristic of Gospel resurrection stories, namely, the commissioning of those who now become apostles. In

[19]This appearance is similar to Luke's story of the two disciples on the road to Emmaus, but once again the wording is not the same.

[20]See the discussion of the meal of bread and fish in John 21:9 (p. 87 below).

The Resurrection in Mark

Mark 16:15 it is both startling and encouraging that those who have just been upbraided for lack of faith and hardness of heart are now entrusted with preaching the gospel to the whole world. What better way to show that God's grace and not human merit is a primary element in the Good News proclaimed by Jesus. By preaching the risen Christ to others, the Eleven will be strengthened in their faith. Jesus' directive, "Going into the whole world, preach the gospel to every creature," is even more comprehensive than the close parallel in Matt 28:19, "Going, make disciples of all nations." Mark 1:1 identified this writing as "The gospel of Jesus Christ, the Son of God"; and it is that gospel with its christological content that is to be preached by the disciples, for it has within itself the power to change all creation. Through this preaching the risen Lord establishes the authority he has won over all things.

The effect of the preaching is described in 16:16: "The person who believes and is baptized will be saved, but the person who does not believe will be condemned." In this the Long Ending resembles Johannine theology wherein Jesus provokes judgment as people are forced to choose between light and darkness: "The person who believes in him is not condemned, but the person who does not believe is condemned already" (John 3:18).[21] The church situation envisaged by the Long Ending is one where those sent out by Jesus carry on his work and the proper response of faith has to be sealed by baptism in order to bring salvation (see 1 Pet 3:21). The harsh fate that punishes the refusal to believe is partially explicable from the indication in the following verse (Mark 16:17) that the preaching of the Gospel will be accompanied by persuasive signs, so that rejection reflects obduracy. Nevertheless, to preach in our times this statement

[21]In John the judgment is in the present time and is provoked by Jesus himself; in the Long Ending the judgment is future and is provoked by those whom Jesus sends out.

The Resurrection in Mark

which dualistically equates belief in Christ with salvation and disbelief with condemnation requires caution. Today disbelief flows from many factors including unconvincing signs, e.g., the proclamation of Christ by some who scarcely resemble him.

In the promise that "Signs will accompany those who believe," Mark 16:17 again is close to Johannine theology: "The one who believes in me will do the works that I do and greater" (John 14:12). These signs show that the power as well as the life of the risen Jesus is given to those who believe in his name. Yet since the proclamation of these disciples is "to all creation," the manifestation of that power is wider than during Jesus' ministry. Of the five signs that Mark 16:17-18 enunciates, only the first (casting out demons) and the last (laying hands on the sick and healing them) were characteristic of the Marcan Jesus' own ministry (Mark 1:25-26; 3:11-12, 22; 7:32-33; 8:25). Prodigies resembling the five signs are portrayed in the accounts in Acts of what the followers of Jesus accomplish after they receive the Holy Spirit and begin their mission. Paul drives out a possessing spirit in Acts 16:16-18. Speaking in new tongues occurs at Pentecost in Acts 2:4-13 (see 10:46). As for picking up serpents and drinking something deadly without harm, one may think of Acts 28:3-6 where a viper fastens on Paul's hand and hangs from it without his suffering harm.[22] Both Peter and Paul use their hands to heal the sick (Acts 3:7; 28:8). Whether or not the composer of the Long Ending knew Acts directly, he certainly knew traditions about how the emissaries of the risen Christ manifested the power that he had over all creation.

The Long Ending of Mark has developed this third appearance at greater length than the first two because the readers derive their faith from the proclamation by the disciples to

---

[22]See also Luke 10:19: "Behold I have given you authority to tread on serpents and scorpions, and over all the power of the enemy; and nothing shall harm you."

The Resurrection in Mark

whom Jesus appeared. The commissioning of these disciples is the concluding action of "the Lord Jesus"[23] on earth; accordingly in 16:19 he is now taken up to heaven and seated at the right of God. Here the Long Ending is close in sequence, but not in wording, to Luke 24:36-52 where, appearing to the Eleven (24:33, 36) in the general context of a meal (24:41), Jesus predicted that there would be preaching in his name to all the nations (24:47), and then having gone out to Bethany, he was taken up to heaven.

The doubts that the disciples once had (Mark 16:13-14) have now been totally overcome, and they obey by going forth and preaching everywhere (16:20). True to his promise the Lord, even though enthroned in heaven, *works with them* confirming "the word" through the signs that follow the disciples.[24] This sense of divine reinforcement was what gave courage to martyrs, as we see in Justin, *Apology* 1.45:

> This mighty word his apostles, going forth from Jerusalem, preached everywhere. And although death is decreed for those who teach or at all confess the name of Christ, we everywhere both embrace and teach it.

[23]There is some textual doubt about this phrase; it would constitute with the dubious Luke 24:3 the only Gospel instances of a title found in Paul and Acts.

[24]This is not far from the description of "the word" in Heb 2:3-4: "Announced first by the Lord, it was attested to us by those who had heard him, while God also witnessed to it by signs and wonders and varied acts of power."

The Resurrection in Mark

Chapter 2

The Resurrection in Matthew (27:62—28:20)

One might assume that a resurrection narrative should start with the women coming to the tomb. Certainly the person who divided the Gospels into chapters felt that way, for in every Gospel that is precisely where a new chapter begins. Thus Matthew 28:1 tells us how Mary Magdalene and the other Mary went to see the sepulcher. In three Gospels I have no quarrel with that manner of beginning resurrection narratives; for what precedes Mark 16:1; Luke 24:1; and John 20:1, respectively, is the story of the burial which is transitional from the crucifixion account to the resurrection.[25] Matthew, however, differs from the others in that, having terminated the burial in 27:61, he has an intervening story in 27:62-66 concerning the guard placed at the sepulcher. That is an integral part of the resurrection story, for elements from it recur in 28:2-4, 11-15; and so we must begin our discussion of the Matthean resurrection narrative not with 28:1, but with 27:62.

That perception is extremely important for understanding the structure of the Matthean narrative. In addition to the transitional episode of the burial that leads to it, four episodes may be distinguished in the narrative: thus a total of five:

(1) [27:57-61: Burial by Joseph of Arimathea, a disciple, with the women present.]

(2) 27:62-66: Chief priests and Pharisees place guards at sepulcher.

(3) 28:1-10: Women come to sepulcher; angel of the Lord descends and frightens the guards, revealing

---

[25]A partial exception is an intermediary half-verse in Luke 23:56b which pertains to the women resting on the Sabbath.

to the women that Jesus is risen; they are to
tell disciples that Jesus is going to Galilee.
Jesus appears to the women.

(4) 28:11-15: Guards bribed by chief priests and assembled
elders to lie that the disciples stole the body.

(5) 28:16-20: Appearance of Jesus to the eleven disciples
and his commissioning them to go to all
nations.

In this structure episodes 1, 3, and 5 concern those favorable
to Jesus: (1) a disciple and the women; (3) the women are to
tell the disciples; (5) appearance to the disciples. Episodes 2
and 4 concern hostile Jewish authorities and the Roman
guards they employ. It is noteworthy that in this artistic arrangement the middle scene (3) mentions all three groups:
the women, the guards, and the disciples. One is encouraged
in this analysis by a detection of the same alternation in the
five-fold structure of episodes in the Matthean infancy narrative.[26] That opening of the Gospel offers many parallels in
thought, wording, and popular motifs to the conclusion of
the Gospel constituted by the resurrection narrative—an inclusion by which Matthew begins and ends in the same way.

[26]The five-part structure of the infancy narrative of Matthew 1:18–2:23 may
be sketched thus:
1. 1:18-25: Revelation by an angel of the Lord to Joseph about Jesus' conception, instructing him to recognize Jesus as his son.
2. 2:1-12: The magi come from the East to worship the King of the Jews, only
to encounter a *hostile* Herod with the chief priests and scribes. The magi
worship Jesus.
3. 2:13-15: Revelation by the angel of the Lord to Joseph to take the child and
his mother to Egypt and thus preserve the child's life.
4. 2:16-18: Herod kills the male children of Bethlehem in an attempt to kill
Jesus.
5. 2:19-23: Revelation by the angel of the Lord to Joseph that those who
sought the child's life are dead and he should return to Nazareth.
Notice that 1, 3, and 5 are positive, while 2 and 4 are negative.

The Resurrection in Matthew

The burial in 27:57-61 was a compassionate action by a disciple, with the women followers of Jesus sitting in attendance opposite the sepulcher; now Matthew turns to malevolent attention paid to the sepulcher. While other Gospels would terminate with the crucifixion scene the hostility by the chief priests and Jewish rulers toward Jesus,[27] Matthew carries it over to the resurrection and uses it to fill in the Sabbath between Jesus' death and burial (late on Friday) and the opening of the tomb (beginning of Sunday). In the infancy narrative that opens Matthew, on hearing of the birth of the King of the Jews, the secular ruler (Herod) worked with the chief priests and the scribes to kill him and thus to prevent even the beginning of his career. At the end of the Gospel, the chief priests and the Pharisees or elders (27:62; 28:12) work with the secular ruler (Pilate) to prevent the survival of his ministry. God will frustrate the armed might of these authorities; and at the end of the resurrection story, as at the end of the infancy story, Jesus emerges triumphant—a lesson of encouragement to Matthew's readers (and to us).

The material in this episode is peculiar to Matthew (even as was the infancy story) and like much popular narrative ignores certain implausibilities. Three times Jesus predicted to his disciples his suffering, violent death, and resurrection on the third day (16:21; 17:22-23; 20:17-19). The disciples never gave evidence of having understood what he meant. Here, however, the chief priests know that Jesus predicted, "After three days I will rise again"; and they understand perfectly what he meant.[28] Consequently, they want the sepulcher made secure until the third day to frustrate Jesus' prophecy. In the

[27]John's postresurrectional "fear of the Jews" is more general; Acts shows the Jewish leaders still hostile towards Peter and Paul.

[28]In Matt 2:3 Herod too was instantly perceptive about the danger presented to him by the birth of the King of the Jews.

The Resurrection in Matthew

25

Sanhedrin trial of Jesus the issues were his ability to destroy the Temple and whether he was the Messiah, the Son of God; but now the interest has shifted to the veracity of the resurrection claim. Jesus is called by his accusers "a deceiver," a description that will become common in later Jewish polemic against him. The skepticism of the authorities, plus their allegation that his disciples will steal the body (repeated in 28:13), suggests that we may have here an issue that Matthew was facing when writing his Gospel. Although during the ministry of Jesus "the chief priests and the Pharisees" were the target of his parable of the vineyard, as the tenants from whom the vineyard would be taken away (Matt 21:45), the Pharisees were noticeably absent during the passion narrative, for they played little direct role in the death of Jesus. They have reappeared here because in the experience of Matthew's church they were the chief opponents and undoubtedly were skeptics about the resurrection of Jesus. This episode has been drawn from a context of apologetics and polemics.

When the core of this popular narrative was taken over into Matthew's Gospel, it gained another dimension: the inability of human power to frustrate God's plan. In their attempt to prevent the resurrection (even if they describe it as a fraud), the chief authorities of the Jews enlist the help of the governing power, addressing their request to Pilate as *kyrios* (Matthean irony). Pilate's affirmative response has often been misunderstood to mean: "You have a guard [of your own]; go and make it secure as you know how." Yet 28:14 suggests that no Jewish guard under the control of the chief priests is meant, for there the priests offer to placate the governor and keep the soldiers of the guard out of trouble. Rather, Pilate's response should be translated: "You have the guard [you just asked for]"—in other words a grant of Roman soldiers. Thus the governing and religious authorities conspire together against the resurrection of Jesus, even

The Resurrection in Matthew

26

as in the infancy narrative Herod conspired with the chief priests and scribes against the life of the Messiah (2:4, 20 ["*Those* who sought the child's life"]). Despite the use of armed force, neither group of earthly powers proves successful. Sealing the stone and setting the guard will be infantile precautions against the power that God is about to release.

EPISODE IN 28:1-10: THE WOMEN AT THE SEPULCHER;
THE ANGEL OF THE LORD AND HIS REVELATION;
JESUS APPEARS TO THE WOMEN

Jesus was often accused of violating the Sabbath; perhaps by deliberate irony Matthew places on the Sabbath the effort of the chief priests and the Pharisees to block the resurrection. As soon as the Sabbath is over (approximately 6:00 P.M. on Saturday) and the first day of the week is beginning, Mary Magdalene and the other Mary set out to see the sepulcher.[29] (Nothing is said about coming to anoint Jesus as in Mark and Luke; the guards, peculiar to Matthew, would never permit that.) What they actually see is a stunning series of events narrated by no other Gospel. First of all there is an earthquake. This is harmonious with what Matthew *alone* described as occurring when Jesus died (27:51b-53): "The earth quaked; and the rocks were split; and the tombs were opened; and many bodies of the saints who had fallen asleep were raised. . . ." Matthew, once more with access to popular storytelling traditions about the resurrection, seeks to convey the wider importance of what God has done for Jesus. In the infancy narrative as "the King of the Jews" was born, his star was visible at its rising (in the East), something seen

[29]An early hour (about dawn) is mentioned in Mark 16:2; Luke 24:1; and John 20:1, although with the contrary indications that "the sun had risen" in Mark and that it was "still dark" in John. There is no such indication in Matthew who has excised both the Marcan references to the morning. What he writes is that the first day of the week was beginning, and by our reckoning that would be about 7:00–8:00 P.M. on Saturday.

The Resurrection in Matthew

by the Gentile magi astronomers. When Jesus died with the charge "The King of the Jews" written on the cross over his head, the earth quaked, pouring the dead out of their tombs, something seen by the Gentile centurion and the soldiers with him. And now to herald Jesus' resurrection the earth quakes once more. The main focus of the passion narrative has been on the role of Jesus in the salvation history of Israel; but Matthew wishes to signal that Jesus' role from birth through death to resurrection is of cosmic importance, shaking the foundations of the world and raising even those long dead.

The vivid and imaginative Matthean description catches the apocalyptic aspect of the resurrection. In addition to the earthquake at the sepulcher, an angel of the Lord descends from heaven and rolls back the stone—once more something peculiar to Matthew. The appearance of the angel fits the apocalyptic context: he is "like lightning," even as the great angel who came to reveal to Daniel the last times had "a face like lightning" (Dan 10:6). His garment is "white as snow," even as Daniel's Ancient of Days who judges the nations had a garment white as snow (Dan 7:9; cf. Mt 17:2). The power of God has intervened definitively at the sepulcher of Jesus, and before it the human powers who had conspired to frustrate the resurrection are as nothing. In fear the guards are shaken even as the earth was, and they become "as if they were dead" (28:4). This is truly ironical: Jesus lives and those set to prevent that are as if dead.

The first action of the angel of the Lord whose arrival has been heralded by the earthquake is to roll back the stone and thus undo the ineffectual sealing placed on it by the order of the chief priests (27:66). Some scholars have thought that Matthew is implying that the resurrection took place at this moment, or (more soberly, since he does not mention the resurrection here) that his popular source described the resurrection at this moment. In fact, the second-century,

The Resurrection in Matthew

apocryphal *Gospel of Peter* (9:35–10:42) places a highly imaginative description of the resurrection precisely at this juncture. Probably, however, *Peter* represents a more developed dramatization of the type of popular account that influenced Matthew. Matthew's silence about the resurrection itself, similar to the silence in the other canonical Gospels, suggests that in more sophisticated circles it was understood that the resurrection could not be described, for it was an event that touched the other world beyond time and space.[30] When Matthew's angel rolls back the stone, he does so not to provide an exit for the resurrection but to make it possible to see that Jesus was no longer in the place where he once lay (28:6) and that therefore the resurrection had already taken place.

The next task of Matthew's "angel of the Lord" is to interpret the emptiness of the sepulcher. The title that Matthew uses for this angel interpreter[31] reminds us that "the angel of the Lord" served as a revealer and interpreter in the Matthean infancy narrative as well. There (but not since) the angel of the Lord appeared three times. First, in 1:20 this angel explained that Mary's pregnancy (which otherwise would have been misinterpreted) stemmed from the Holy Spirit. So also here the angel explains that the empty sepulcher (which "the Jews" will misinterpret as a result of stealing the body) stems from Jesus' having been raised from the dead (28:7). In his second and third appearances in the Matthean infancy narrative (2:13, 19), the angel of the Lord told Joseph what to do in response to the tremendous events that had taken place. So also here the angel of the Lord gives the women

[30]What is entirely in this world and not beyond time and space is the empty tomb, and that is described on the first day of the week by all four evangelists.

[31]Luke 24:22-23 makes clear that the "two men" (*andres*) of 24:4 were angels; John 20:12 has two angels. Mark 16:5 speaks of a "young man" (*neaniskos*) who in my judgment is to be interpreted as an angel.

The Resurrection in Matthew

instruction to go quickly and tell the disciples that Jesus has been raised. Those disciples of Jesus foresook him and fled when he was arrested (26:56); and Peter, the one exception who hesitantly tried to continue with Jesus by following at a distance (26:58), denied him three times and cursed him (26:69-75, especially 26:74). Yet they are still in God's plan and are to receive the revelation about the resurrection from the women. These women (whom Matthew does *not* call disciples), although present at Golgotha, hitherto had only the passive role of looking on the death of Jesus from afar (27:55) and sitting opposite the sepulcher when he was buried (27:61). Now they are rewarded for their initiative in coming to see the sepulcher by being made the first human proclaimers of the resurrection[32] and the intermediaries through whom the faith of the disciples will be rekindled. Many phrases in this description ("Do not be afraid"; "Go quickly"; "They departed quickly . . . fear and great joy") stem from the stereotypic language of angelic announcements in the Old Testament and are found also in the angelic announcements of the infancy narratives.[33] Nevertheless, Matthew is surely presenting virtues that his Christian readers should imitate in receiving and sharing the news of the risen Lord; they are being invited to go quickly with reverential fear and great joy to tell others.

In a further reward to the women who are joyfully obedient to the angel, Jesus himself appears to them. If we may judge from 1 Corinthians 15:5ff., a list of the appearances of the risen Jesus associated with official preaching (see 1 Cor 15:11-12) concentrated mostly on the apostolic recipients

---

[32]Matt 28:7 has the women instructed to tell the disciples, "He has been raised from the dead," an element absent from the instruction to them in Mark 16:7. The concluding clause in the instruction of Matthew 28:7 adds solemnity: "Behold, I have told you."

[33]R. E. Brown, *The Birth of the Messiah* (Garden City, New York: Doubleday, 1977) 155-59, 341.

The Resurrection in Matthew

(Cephas [Peter], the Twelve, James, Paul); but that does not mean that the other appearances did not occur or were not remembered. Indeed in popular circles, appearances to those who were not part of church leadership may have been of great interest and have received vivid narrative development. In any case, John 20:11-18 (in a more developed form), Mark 16:9, and Matthew 28:9-10 record an appearance to Mary Magdalene (and in Matthew to "the other Mary" 28:1).[34] The reaction of the women to the sight of the risen Jesus is interesting. They come up (a verb Matthew often uses for an action expressing awe) and worship him. Certainly in that reaction they serve as a model for how Christians should respect the presence of the Lord. Furthermore, they clutch his feet (in the Johannine parallel Jesus has to warn Mary Magdalene, "Do not cling to me"). While such a gesture may underline the reality of Jesus' body and thus have an apologetic function, it also expresses human affection for Jesus—probably an important element in popular appearance narratives. Jesus' message to the women repeats that given to them by the angel. Seemingly, then, in these nonapostolic appearances revelation was not an important factor. Nevertheless, a minor element in the message in 28:10 is interesting. While the angel told the women to report to Jesus' disciples (28:7), here the message is to go to Jesus' *brothers*. A new status will emerge for those who hear and believe in the resurrection: they become God's children and thus the brothers and sisters of Jesus.[35]

[34]Because Matt 28:9-10 is heavily Matthean in style, there have been attempts to deny that there was preGospel tradition behind this appearance and to explain it simply as creative Matthean filling out of Marcan silence. Since I find no compelling evidence that John's account of a similar appearance is a rewriting of Mark, it is far easier to suppose a preGospel tradition that each evangelist has rewritten in his own way.

[35]See also John 20:17 (p. 72 below) for the use of "brothers" for disciples (20:18), and Matt 12:49; 25:40.

The Resurrection in Matthew

Matthew now returns to the story of the guard, just as in the infancy narrative he resumed the story of Herod after he had stopped to tell how the magi frustrated Herod's plan. Although the chief priests hear all that had taken place and therefore how an angel of the Lord descended from heaven and opened the sepulcher, they do not cease their opposition; they do not repent and come to believe. Earlier (26:3-5,14-15) the chief priests and elders gathered and took counsel on how to arrest Jesus secretly and kill him; and they paid Judas silver pieces to hand Jesus over. They also sought false testimony to convict Jesus (26:59). A similar process of paying silver pieces and using falsehood is followed here. (One may wonder whether Matthew does not hint at their future punishment, for the silver pieces they paid to Judas came back to haunt them [27:5-6]; and the silver paid to the guards is not much nobler than the blood money paid to Judas.) The last mention of these Jewish authorities (28:15) has them *teaching* the soldiers to lie; the last mention of Jesus (28:20) will have him telling his disciples to teach all nations whatever he has commanded.

This picture of plotting, a bribe, deliberate falsehood, and a promise to placate is surely a reflection of popular prejudice showing how early Christians attributed malevolence to those who opposed them. While in individual instances of such opposition to Christians there may indeed have been malevolence, Matthew's hostile use of "the Jews" is a generalization that goes beyond historical incidents and reflects antagonism and rumors circulating among ordinary folk. In the more sensitive interreligious relations of our own times, such a broad portrayal of the Jewish authorities as scheming liars and the generalization of the lie as one circulated among "the Jews" should make Christians uneasy. But the period in which this

The Resurrection in Matthew

harsh polemic was developed did not share our sensitivities. We have clear instances of Jews hating other Jews over religious issues; the Essenes pictured the Sadducee high priest at Jerusalem as one who embodied deceit; and the high priest did not hesitate to crucify Pharisees and seek to kill the Essene leader. If Acts is to be believed, Jewish authorities would have been pleased to have Christian apostles like Peter and Paul executed. In such a context, when a false explanation of the empty tomb of Jesus circulated among some Jews, it is understandable (even if not to be approved) that ordinary Christians would universalize the attitude and regard it as a knowing falsehood. Indeed, if one may judge from the apocryphal *Gospel of Peter* 8:28–11:49,[36] that bitterness toward Jews in less-controlled, popular Christian circles was stronger than what appears in the more formalized canonical Gospels. One aspect of Matthew's story remains an important lesson. He is implying the futility of the nasty apologetics that has developed in some Jewish circles against the resurrection. Christians may learn that hostile apologetics on either side is futile and does little to further the religious cause that one deems right.

EPISODE IN 28:16-20: THE APPEARANCE OF JESUS
TO THE DISCIPLES ON A MOUNTAIN IN GALILEE

The final scene shifts from Jerusalem to Galilee—the "Galilee of the Gentiles" as Matthew 4:15 describes the land where Jesus began his ministry and first called his disciples (4:18-22). Jesus had predicted at the beginning of the passion that, although the disciples would be scattered, after he was raised up he would go before them to Galilee (26:32). The Galilee directive was reiterated at the sepulcher both by the angel of

[36]There the Jewish elders and scribes are themselves at the tomb and therefore seemingly observe the opening of the tomb and the resurrection itself. They acknowledge themselves guilty of great sin before God in concocting a lie about this, but they persuade Pilate to join in.

The Resurrection in Matthew

the Lord and by the risen Jesus (28:7, 10) with the added promise that there the disciples (now become his "brothers") would see him. Now at "the mountain" he fulfills the promise. Matthew does not think of a specific geographical mountain but rather of the mountain where Jesus sat when he taught the disciples the Sermon on the Mount (5:1) and the mountain where he was transfigured before Peter, James, and John (17:1). Just as on Mount Sinai or Horeb, Moses encountered God and received from him the Law, so on a mountain during the ministry the disciples had seen the glory of God in the transfigured Jesus and received from him an interpretation of the Law: "You have heard it said but I say to you."[37] The disciples who now come to this mountain once more have already learned from the women that here they are to see Jesus. It is not surprising, then, that despite their dismal history of failure in the passion, they worship the risen Jesus as soon as they see him (28:17), even as the women had done (28:9). At the beginning of the gospel the Gentile magi came and fell down and worshiped him; at the end his Jewish followers (the women) and disciples render the same worship.

The motif of doubt recurs frequently in appearances of Jesus recounted in the various Gospels; and here while all the disciples worship, some doubt. These are members of the Twelve (or with Matthew's greater precision, of the Eleven); they heard Jesus' threefold prediction of the resurrection during his ministry; they heard his promise to go before them to Galilee, and they heard that promise reiterated by the women; yet some doubt. This doubt may have an apologetic dimension, showing that even the disciples were not anxious to believe and were certainly not credulous; they had to be convinced. More important, the doubt would remind the readers that, even after the resurrection, faith is not a facile response. It might also encourage them that Jesus is not

[37]See Matt 5:21-22, 27-28, 31-32, 33-34, 38-39, 43-44.

The Resurrection in Matthew

repelled by doubt, for he now comes close to the disciples to speak. Doubting or not, they have worshiped him, and he responds to them.

If appearance stories point back by insisting that the risen one is truly the Jesus who was crucified and buried, some of them also point forward to the mission that the resurrection must produce, reflecting an insistence on sharing with others what God has done. Scholars recognize this by speaking of church-founding appearances. In Mark 16:14-15, Matthew, Luke, and John there is such an appearance to members of the Twelve that makes them apostles, i.e., those sent to proclaim the resurrection. The sending is based on Jesus' own status, showing that as Jesus carried on God's work, the apostles carry on Jesus' work. This relationship is phrased in Matthew 28:18-19: "All authority [or power] in heaven and on earth has been given to me; go therefore. . . ."[38] Such wording echoes Dan 7:14 where authority is given in heaven by the Ancient of Days to a son of man "so that peoples of all nations and languages would serve him." Thus the eschatological and apocalyptic atmosphere established by the earthquake and the appearance of the angel of the Lord at the sepulcher continues on the mountain in Galilee. The authority of the church is delegated from Jesus who has been elevated[39] and has authority in heaven and on earth; the mission that flows from it will touch all na-

[38] The functional equivalent is John 20:21, "As the Father has sent me, so do I send you." Notice that the sayings of the risen Jesus tend to be parallel in meaning and function but not in words. This raises the issue of whether the postresurrectional revelations were in words or by detectable intention that found different wording in different communities. As I point out in *Virginal Conception* (note 1 above) 107-8, this is not a point on which one can have surety.

[39] Although Matthew does not use the language of elevation, one may suppose that here, as elsewhere in the NT, resurrection concerns more than a point of departure (from the sepulcher or tomb); it involves a destination, namely, to glory with God.

The Resurrection in Matthew

tions. It is entrusted to the Eleven, even though some doubted. We are left to suspect that the word of Jesus solved the doubt, and that by proclaiming to others, their faith was strengthened.

The wording of the mission given to the Eleven is significant: "Going therefore, make disciples of all nations." Jesus already had authority during his public ministry (7:29; 9:8; 11:27; 21:23); but when he sent the Twelve out at that time (10:5-6), he instructed them: "Go *not* among the nations [Gentiles], and enter no town of the Samaritans; but go rather to the lost sheep of the house of Israel." Now the risen Jesus with full eschatological power ("All authority") sends them out to all the nations. Israel is not excluded (see 23:34); but the progression in these two commands, one in the ministry and one after the resurrection, embodies the experience of Matthean Christianity. Jesus himself spoke only to Jews (15:24); and at first so did those who had been with him in the public ministry as they went out after the resurrection to proclaim the kingdom. Yet in the first two decades of church development they discovered that the plan of God was wider.[40] At the beginning of the Gospel Matthew signaled the wide extension of God's plan by writing of Gentile magi who came to Jerusalem—the fulfillment of an Old Testament dream (Isa 2:2-4). Now, however, it becomes clear that the apostles cannot simply wait for the Gentiles to come; they must go out to them. And if in the ministry the chief Jewish followers of Jesus (the Twelve) were called disciples, that privilege and title is to be extended to all nations.

This mission to make disciples of the nations is to be accompanied and accomplished by baptism. Elsewhere in the New Testament baptism is in the name of Jesus (Acts 2:38; 10:48; 1 Cor 6:11; etc.); but here at the end of that Gospel which the subsequent church made her own catechism we find the triadic formula: "In the name of the Father, and of

[40]See the dramatization of this for Peter in Acts 10.

The Resurrection in Matthew

the Son, and of the Holy Spirit''—undoubtedly the formula in use in Matthew's community when he wrote. Instances in Paul and elsewhere show that very quickly believers in Jesus acknowledged that God the Father was the source and goal of all that Jesus said and did. The Holy Spirit was quickly related to the continuance of Jesus' work within the believer and within the church. Thus while belief in Jesus (his name, who he was) was the first essential component of baptismal profession, the Father and the Spirit were brought into that confession to articulate the larger picture to which believers committed themselves. By a century after Matthew's time an expansion of articulated belief about the Father, the Son, and the Holy Spirit produced a creed divided into articles centered on those three divine agents. This baptismal creed of the Roman church we know as the Apostles' Creed. In other words, the Matthean formula which seems to stand at the terminus of New Testament baptismal development also represents a beginning in the custom of professing at baptism a formula that enshrines what Christians believe the triune God has done. This formula describes the fullness of divine action to which the acceptance of baptism is the response.

The baptizing of the nations by the disciples is to be accompanied by their teaching all that Jesus had commanded. Several times Matthew has summed up Jesus' activity in terms of his teaching (4:23; 9:35; 11:1), and that task is now passed on to the Eleven. Their teaching is not to be new or their own, but "all that I commanded you." This is Exodus language (7:2; 23:22; etc.) for what God commanded Israel and so is perfectly appropriate in the final directive of the lawgiver of the new covenant.

The solemn last words of Jesus in Matthew (28:20), "Behold, I am with you all days to the end of time [*aiōn:* age, world],"[41] echo the first words ever spoken about him in the

[41]The eschatological sweep of the last words of Jesus is brought out by the

The Resurrection in Matthew

beginning of the Gospel (1:23), "Behold the virgin shall conceive and bear a son and they will name him Emmanuel, which means 'God with us.'" The resurrection is for Matthew evidence not only that God was with Jesus who conquered death, but also that in Jesus God's abiding presence is with all those who are baptized in the name of the Father, and of the Son, and of the Holy Spirit and who observe all that Jesus has commanded, as taught by the disciples. In Isa 41:10 God promised his people Israel: "Do not be afraid: I am with you." Here the promise is reiterated to an enlarged people including Gentiles who have come to know Him in Jesus Christ. Earthly powers represented by the secular ruler, the chief priests, and the scribes/elders tried to prevent the plan of God both at the conception/birth of Jesus and at his crucifixion/resurrection. They were unsuccessful then, and they will be equally unsuccessful in preventing it till the end of time.[42]

repetition of "all": "all authority"; "all nations"; "all that I command"; and "all days."

[42] In 17:17 Jesus asked a faithless and perverse generation, "How long am I to be with you?" Here he answers that question for those who are his disciples: "all days."

The Resurrection in Matthew

Chapter 3

The Resurrection in Luke (24:1-53; Acts 1:1-12)

The most architectonic of the evangelists, Luke gives a geographical framework to his expansive two-volume narrative of Jesus and of the Spirit. The narrative begins in the Jerusalem Temple among Jews (Luke 1:5-8) and ends in Rome with the directive that future evangelization should concentrate on the Gentiles (Acts 28:28). The hinge that joins the story of Jesus from Nazareth to the story of the Spirit who guides the mission to the ends of the earth is a crucial series of events that take place in Jerusalem, namely, Jesus' passion, death, resurrection, and sending of the Spirit. The first part of that hinge series (Jesus' passion and death) is recounted at the end of Luke's first volume (Gospel of Luke 22-23); the last part of the hinge series (sending of the Spirit) is recounted at the beginning of Luke's second volume (Acts 2). The resurrection, involving appearances of the risen Jesus in Jerusalem,[43] is so pivotal, however, that it is recounted both at the end of the Gospel and the beginning of Acts. As a Jerusalem event at the end of the Gospel, it constitutes an inclusion with the beginning of that Gospel, so that the story both starts and ends in the Jerusalem Temple (see Luke 24:53). As a Jerusalem event at the beginning of Acts, it functions as a counterpoise to the ending in Rome, so that the book becomes a story of how Christianity moved from Jerusalem to Rome, from Jews to Gentiles.

A further indication of the import of the Jerusalem setting of the Lucan resurrection account is found when we consider the geographical motif of journey that governs almost two-thirds of the Lucan Gospel. We hear in Luke 9:51: "When

---

[43]Luke is the only Gospel that has no room for appearances in Galilee, an especially significant fact if one thinks that Luke knew Mark (16:7).

the days approached for his being taken up, he set his face to go to Jerusalem." One can distinguish three stages in this great journey to Jerusalem. (I) The movement from Galilee to Jerusalem runs from 9:51 to 19:27 (with reminders in 10:38; 13:22; 17:11; 18:31). (II) The entry into Jerusalem and a rejection there (particularly at the Temple) that eventually causes Jesus to be put to death on the cross runs from 19:28 to 23:56. (III) The raising of Jesus and his being taken from this world to heaven culminates the Gospel (24:1-53) and is reused to open Acts (1:1-12) so that the heavenly ascent is described twice (Luke 24:51; Acts 1:9). The journey of Jesus from Galilee to Jerusalem ends in heaven; that constitutes a promise that the journey of his disciples to the ends of the earth (Acts 1:8) will also end in heaven.

Giving more detailed attention to this last stage involving the resurrection and ascension, we find that from the viewpoint of time it consists of two sections, while geographically there are four episodes:

A. Easter Sunday Events
   (1) 24:1-12: The women and Peter visit the empty tomb.
   (2) 24:13-35: Two disciples going to Emmaus encounter Jesus.
   (3) 24:36-53: Jesus appears to the Eleven gathered in Jerusalem and is taken to heaven from Bethany; they return to Jerusalem, blessing God in the Temple.
B. Appearances during Forty Days
   (4) Acts 1:1-12: Jesus instructs the apostles to wait in Jerusalem for the Spirit but ultimately to be his witnesses to the end of the earth; he is taken to heaven from Mount Olivet.

In the course of considering the episodes one by one, we shall be sorely tempted to compare Luke to Mark in Episode 1 to observe the Lucan adaptations, and to compare Luke to John in Episode 3 since only these two Gospels share an Easter Sunday evening appearance of Jesus to the disciples

The Resurrection in Luke

gathered in Jerusalem. Nevertheless throughout this volume I have to read each Gospel as a unit without intrusive appeals to other Gospels for knowledge that the Gospel under consideration does not convey. This insistence allows us to hear the Gospel in a way that resembles how the first audience must have heard it since they scarcely had the comparative material supplied by the other Gospels. It also facilitates appreciation of the inner consistency of the Lucan Gospel, especially of how the resurrection chapter (24) echoes motifs in the chapters (1–2) dealing with the infancy.

EPISODE IN LUKE 24:1-12:
VISITS TO THE EMPTY TOMB

Although Luke begins the account on the first day of the week (24:1), his opening picks up on a transitional sentence that concluded the burial. Luke told us not only that the Galilean women saw how Jesus' body was laid in the tomb (23:55) but also that they went back to prepare spices and myrrh and then rested on the Sabbath according to the commandment (23:56).[44] In reporting that, while Luke did not identify by name the women from Galilee, he made their good intentions amply clear. They did not assist in the burial because they had at hand no prepared spices, and their delay until Sunday was dictated by their obedience to the commandment of Sabbath rest. Luke's story of Jesus' birth was replete with references to how those involved were law-observant (1:6, 8-9; 2:21-25, 37, 39, 41-42), and that motif returns at his death. From the beginning to the end of Jesus' life on earth, there was no break with the commandments that God had given to the people of Israel.[45]

---

[44]Functionally, then, both Luke and Matthew interpose a Sabbath event between Jesus' burial on Friday and the finding of the empty tomb on Sunday; but Matthew's story of obtaining a guard for the tomb (27:62-66) is long enough to constitute an episode in itself.

[45]Eventually Luke will come to the issue of Christian non-observance of the

The Resurrection in Luke

The fact that the women come at the crack of dawn on the first day after the Sabbath with the spices they had prepared (24:1) catches their eagerness to render loving service. In describing the growing perplexity of these women when they reach and enter the tomb, Luke makes an elegant play on their finding what they did not expect (the tomb open, for the stone had been rolled back—Luke's first mention of the stone!) and their not finding what they did expect (the body of the Lord Jesus). Fear is added to perplexity when suddenly there are standing alongside them two angelic men in dazzling apparel.[46] At the beginning of the Gospel (Luke 2:9) an angel of the Lord was suddenly standing alongside the shepherds to explain the significance of what had happened at Bethlehem; at the end the same divine assistance is supplied to explain the significance of what had happened at the Place of the Skull (Calvary) and at the tomb. The birth of Jesus brought joy; the death brought sorrow; but both are manifestations of divine glory (see 24:26). Fearful (24:5), even as were the shepherds (2:9), the women bow to the ground. The question the two "men" address to the women, "Why do you seek the living among the dead?", is a rhetorical revelation that despite the crucifixion Jesus lives. In the better manuscripts of Luke the angels go on to a more prosaic proclamation: "He is not here but has been raised." That Jesus is not here the women can see with their eyes; that this is because God has raised Jesus they must take on faith. The two angels go on to rebuke implicitly the women's lack of spontaneous understanding that resurrection had to be the denouement of crucifixion: in Galilee Jesus had given a detailed outline of the fate of the Son of Man, including

food laws. On that issue Peter will be instructed by new divine revelation in Acts 10:9-16; even then, however, partial and respectful observance will be included in Acts 15:29.

[46] Although Luke 24:4 speaks of "two men," their clothing suggests heavenly origin; and 24:23 identifies them as angels. See Acts 10:30; Dan 8:15.

The Resurrection in Luke

resurrection on the third day.[47] Moreover, since Jesus' words involved a "must," that fate was divinely ordained—an ordination that made the passion intelligible and the resurrection inevitable.

Brought to recall Jesus' prediction (24:8), the women show they have spontaneity by immediately acting. That Jesus lives is the heart of the Gospel, and the good news can never simply be received and kept. The women go back from the tomb to tell the Eleven and "all the rest" (24:9). Luke does not specify who the latter are, but presumably they include the two disciples who are to set out for Emmaus in the next episode. In 24:11 Luke will tell his readers of the contemptuous reception given the women's report; but first (24:10) he stops to identify belatedly these Galilean women who "stood from afar" at the crucifixion, observed the burial, and now with their spices have visited the tomb emptied by the resurrection. Lucan readers should recognize the first named, Mary Magdalene, for alone among the Gospels Luke has introduced her during the public ministry of Jesus. She was one of the women whom Jesus had healed of evil spirits and infirmities; in particular, from Magdalene seven demons had gone out (8:2). The second woman, Joanna, the wife of Chuza, Herod's steward (a possible translation of *epitropos* in 8:3), was one of the same group. (The "Mary of James" listed third by Luke 24:10 has not previously been mentioned, and no identification is given for "the other women.") The fact that Mary Magdalene and Joanna were companions of the Twelve in Galilee (8:1-3) in the following of Jesus makes all the more startling that now their story of the empty tomb and the angelic explanation is treated by the Eleven as if it were silly chatter that need not be believed.[48] The women,

[47]The form given to Jesus' words by the angels in 24:6-7 is an amalgam of several statements by the Lucan Jesus: 9:22, 44; 18:31-33.

[48]Commentaries often explain that generally the testimony of women was not given credence, but the situation here is aggravated because of the close

The Resurrection in Luke

although slow to understand, had believed the explanation of the angelic men who reminded them of Jesus' prediction; the Eleven refuse belief even though the women's account must have reminded them of the prediction. Luke 24:10 underlines their obduracy by reporting that the women "kept telling" the apostles about what had happened—an unusual touch in a Gospel that is so gentle on the Twelve/Eleven.

A footnote to this episode is supplied by 24:12 which reports that one of the Eleven, Peter (evidently deciding to test the women's story), ran to the tomb to peer in.[49] The fact that Peter sees only the burial wrappings[50] and not the body of Jesus confirms at least part of the women's story. Yet Peter is not said to have concluded that the other part of their story was true, namely, that Jesus had been raised from the dead; for he returns from the tomb not with joy but with amazement. Did the fact that he did not see angelic men there make him doubt? The rest of the chapter will be devoted by Luke to appearances of the risen Jesus that will overcome disbelief among the Eleven and "all the rest" who were with them. And in a passing reference (24:34) we shall hear that Peter (Simon) was the recipient of a special appearance.

past relationship of the apostles to these women. According to Luke 24:34 the Eleven did accept the report of Simon (Peter); yet Peter had seen the risen Lord and these women had not.

[49] This verse is found both in the best copies and the oldest manuscript of Luke. It should not be omitted despite verbal similarity to John 20:3-4. A later passage, Luke 24:24, suggests that Peter was not alone: "Some of those who were with us went off to the tomb and found it just as the women said."

[50] Earlier (23:53) Luke reported that Jesus was wrapped in a shroud (sindōn); here he speaks of burial wrappings (othonia). Even if Luke derived these reports from different sources, readers would be meant to see the terms as equivalent, or to think of the shroud as part of the burial wrappings.

The Resurrection in Luke

TWO DISCIPLES ON THE ROAD TO EMMAUS

In many ways this story, very Lucan in style, has no parallel among the other Gospels.[51] The longest of all the canonical resurrection stories, its length provides the risen Jesus an opportunity to offer revelatory teaching that shows how the entire passion and resurrection fit into God's plan contained in the Scriptures. A connection with the first episode (the women and Peter at the tomb) is established by the information that the second occurs on the same day and that the dramatis personae are "two of them," i.e., of those who had heard the women's story and refused to believe.[52] (Perhaps disbelief is illustrated by their decision to leave Jerusalem despite the report that the Lord had risen there.) The naming of Emmaus as their destination and the specification of the distance as seven miles (60 stadia) lend realism to the story—even if those details have caused interpreters trouble ever since in identifying a plausible place that would jibe with the distance.[53]

Picturesque too is Luke's having the two men discussing "all these things that had occurred [in relation to Jesus]" at the very instant that "Jesus himself" appears to them

[51]Scholars classify it as a tale, or legend, or circumstantial narrative. Leaving aside the pejorative tone in some of those classifications, we must recognize dramatization in the Lucan narrative. The only parallel in storyline is in the Marcan Appendix (16:12-13): "After these things [the appearance to Magdalene; her report to those who had been with him], he appeared in another form to two of them walking, going into the country. Having gone back, they announced it to the rest; but they did not believe them." Some would argue that this is close to the pre-Gospel tradition that Luke dramatized.

[52]Only in 24:18, with the naming of one of them as Cleopas, does it become clear that these are not members of the Eleven.

[53]Some manuscripts and Church Fathers read "160 stadia" (=18.4 miles), a distance comparable to the 20 miles from Jerusalem to Amwas (Ammaous Nicopolis) near Latrun. There is rabbinic evidence suggesting the presence of Christians at Emmaus.

The Resurrection in Luke

(24:14-15). It is a dramatic moment when the main figure of all these episodes, who thus far has been the subject of revelation and discussion, at last comes on the scene, and even more dramatic because he is not recognized. That the risen Jesus is different is noted in several Gospels (pp. 19, 71, 84), but Luke's way of explaining it relates the problem to the disciples whose "eyes were held back from recognizing him" (24:16). By the casual atmosphere he gives to the encounter, Luke implies how the two must have looked on Jesus: happening by, perhaps a Passover pilgrim (24:18) leaving Jerusalem to return home, and wanting to share their company on the road, he shows interest in their conversation. When they start to answer him, they stop walking and confront him with dismay, as Cleopas[54] demands rhetorically how this man, who has been in Jerusalem, can be so singularly ignorant of what has been happening there. The simple artistic staging of the episode continues in 24:19 as the stranger asks "What things?", opening the way for a dramatic recounting of the passion of Jesus of Nazareth,[55] "a prophetic man mighty in deed and word before God and all the people" (24:19-20). In his first public appearance at Nazareth, Jesus spoke of himself as a prophet (4:24); later as Jesus set himself to go to Jerusalem the reason he offered was that no prophet should perish at a distance from Jerusalem (13:33); here his followers clearly acknowledge him to have had that role. Yet

[54]Perhaps Luke considered it dramatic to postpone the naming of characters in these episodes until the narrative is advanced (only in 24:10 were the women named). The many attempts to name the other disciple (e.g., Peter) are in vain and counter-productive to the Lucan emphasis in the story.

[55]The concise summary of the passion (with parallels in the sermons in Acts, e.g., 2:22-23) has the statement: "Our chief priests and rulers gave him over to a sentence of death, and they crucified him." It refutes the claim that, because Luke's account of the Jewish trial of Jesus has no formal sentence of condemnation (22:71), Luke did not blame the Jewish authorities for the death of Jesus (see also Acts 2:36; 3:13; 4:10). Typically Lucan is the contrast between the authorities (negative) and "all the people" (positive).

The Resurrection in Luke

46

(unusual for Luke) there is also a note of disillusionment: "We were hoping that he was the one who was going to redeem Israel"—a disappointment all the more startling when we remember that Zechariah, father of the Baptist, had praised God: "He has visited and accomplished redemption for His people" (1:68); and Anna, having seen the child Jesus, spoke of him to all who were awaiting the redemption of Israel (2:38). Cleopas, who gives voice to this disappointment about Jesus, is one of those who were with the Eleven when Magdalene and the other women reported the resurrection of Jesus (24:9), and previously the Eleven had been congratulated by Jesus for having continued with him in his trials (22:28). The cross has turned fidelity into discouragement! Yet the women's message was not totally without effect, for Cleopas mentions it as a counterindication to the loss of hope. The women were reminded by the two angels that Jesus had said the Son of Man would rise on the third day (24:7), and this is the third day (24:21). Cleopas then recounts the substance of the first episode involving the visit of the women and of "some of those who were with us" to the empty tomb (24:22-24)[56]—all this with a glimmer of hope but no real faith.

Still unrecognized, the stranger begins to answer the implicit objections to believing that Jesus was the redeemer of Israel (24:25)—not objections raised by the enemies of Jesus among the Jewish authorities but objections raised by those who have been following him. Those who are "foolish and slow of heart to believe all the prophets had foretold" are disciples! The "all" is in one way typical Lucan generalization (see Acts 24:14), but in another way it was only by com-

---

[56]In the present sequence 24:22-24 is a summary of what has already been narrated, but some scholars see it as the kind of nucleus that Luke developed into the longer narrative. Although Mark 16:1-8 does not mention the appearance of Jesus (to the women) at the tomb, only Luke explicitly excludes appearances at the tomb.

The Resurrection in Luke

bining various passages from the prophets[57] that Christians could reconcile with God's plan their picture of a suffering Messiah who was also exalted (24:26: "the Messiah had to suffer these things and [so] to enter his glory"). Already at the beginning of the Gospel (Luke 3:22) the combination of a messianic exaltation psalm (Ps 2:7) and a Suffering Servant passage (Isa 42:1) implicitly set the pattern for this, as God spoke about Jesus at the baptism. The theme of a Messiah having to suffer first will continue in Luke 24:46 and in the Christian preaching of Acts 3:18; 17:3; 26:23. Evidently the idea that one crucified as a wrongdoer could be a glorious king was very difficult for the early Christians to accept—in preChristian Judaism there was no clear expectation of a suffering Messiah—and so it was a focal point in hermeneutical reflections on the Jewish Scriptures.[58] While we can be certain that in the explanations offered by the risen Jesus from 24:25 on, we are hearing phrases from early Christian preaching about Jesus, Luke would suggest strongly that Jesus himself initiated this use of Scripture, beginning with Moses and all the prophets to articulate his understanding of

[57]Luke/Acts uses a Jewish designation for the biblical books (the Law and the Prophets; see 24:27) wherein what we call the historical books (from Joshua through Kings) are the Former Prophets, and the writing prophets are the Latter Prophets. Thus the dynastic oracle in 2 Sam 7:11-16, promising an eternal throne to the kings of the House of David (the basis of the expectation of "the Messiah" understood as the unique or final anointed Davidic king) and the Isaian description of the Suffering Servant (Israel, but understood by Christians to be Jesus) would be part of what "all the prophets" had foretold.

[58]Early Christians shared contemporary Jewish hermeneutics whereby the prophets were thought to have spoken of the distant future, specifically of what was now happening. For Christians it was not so much that the Scriptures were thought to throw light on Jesus; rather Jesus was thought to bring out the meaning of the Scriptures. While undoubtedly some of the arguments based on Scripture were honed in debates with non-believing Jews, the primary goal in appealing to the Scriptures was to supply understanding to believers.

The Resurrection in Luke

himself (24:27). As can be seen from the description of the Teacher of Righteousness in the Dead Sea Scrolls, such a proceeding would be normal for a Jewish religious figure of the time.

Luke's admirable storytelling technique is apparent in 24:28-29 as the disciples struggle to get this intriguing stranger to stay with them at the village of Emmaus, to dine and spend the night. His opening up of the Scriptures during the journey may have made their hearts burn within them (as they acknowledge later in 24:32), but they still have not recognized him. Yet their appeal for him "to stay" shows that they have not lost the instinct of discipleship, and now at table with them Jesus makes the gesture of breaking bread that finally opens their eyes. As soon as they recognize that it is Jesus, he disappears from their sight (24:31). From analogies in their own mythology, pagan readers of this story would surely grasp that a divine figure had disguised himself and visited with mortals. Luke's Christian readers, however, are to learn more from the episode, as the commentary supplied by the two disciples (speaking to each other in 24:32 or to the Eleven in 24:35) makes clear.

First, even though exposition of the Scriptures by Jesus did not bring about recognition, reflection on the Scriptural exposition set their hearts on fire and prepared them for recognition. Second, they recognized him in the breaking of the bread. While one may contend that Jesus had a characteristic way of doing this so that the disciples were recognizing a familiar style, more is involved. Whether used nominally or verbally, breaking bread is a Lucan expression (Acts 2:42, 46; 20:7, 11; 27:35) generally thought to refer to a eucharistic meal. That connotation here is strengthened by the similarity in describing what Jesus did at the last meal (Last Supper) that he ate with his disciples and what he does here. Comparing the two, we see the plausibility that Luke wanted his readers to understand that it was in a eucharistic action that Jesus was recognized:

The Resurrection in Luke

22:19: "Having taken bread, having given thanks [*eucharistein*], he broke and gave it to them, saying, 'This is my body which is given for you.'"

24:30: "Having taken bread, he blessed (it or God); and having broken, he gave it about to them."

(The issue is not whether Jesus actually celebrated a eucharist with the two disciples at Emmaus but how Luke is using the story to instruct his readers.)

Taken in this way, the episode in 24:13-35 would have supplied important instruction. These readers might have reflected to themselves nostalgically that a half-century before in a nearby land there were people fortunate enough to have seen the risen Jesus with their own eyes: "Would that we had been there!" Luke is reporting that those who were in that enviable situation and saw him could not truly know Jesus until the Scriptures were expounded and they recognized him in the eucharistic meal. The Christians of Luke's time had the Scriptures and the breaking of the bread—those same means of knowing the Lord. So have Christians ever since, for the Scriptures and the eucharist are the essential components of our Sunday service. In the matter of encountering the risen Jesus *with faith,* a past generation is not more privileged than the present one.

***

As a transition from this episode to the next, Luke 24:33 recounts that "at that same hour" when Jesus disappeared, the two disciples returned to Jerusalem where they found gathered together "the Eleven and those with them." We remember that when the women came back from the tomb after encountering the angelic men, they made their report to "the Eleven and all the rest" (24:9). At the end of these first two episodes Luke illustrates the duty of sharing "the good news" of the risen Lord with others, while at the same time

The Resurrection in Luke

showing the centrality of the apostles in Jerusalem who are now about to see the risen Lord themselves.[59]

The truly curious factor is that before the two disciples can make their report, the Eleven have their own news: "In reality the Lord has been raised and has appeared to Simon" (24:34).[60] The "in reality" means that the Eleven presume that the two returning disciples know no more than when they left, namely, that both the women and Peter had found an empty tomb and that the women claimed to have seen angels who announced that Jesus was risen. All doubts that the Eleven had about those earlier reports have been resolved while the two disciples were away, for the Lord has been seen by Simon (Peter). Surely Luke is combining different traditions here, and the sentence that affirms the appearance to Simon may be a form of the very old preaching formula found in 1 Cor 15:5 which lists the appearance to Cephas (Peter) first. But in the present sequence the sentence has the effect of showing that the apostolic faith in the risen Lord is not based on a story about an empty tomb or even on the message of angels; it is based on an actual encounter with Jesus. The two disciples may have known the risen Lord because they recognized him in the breaking of the bread, but Simon (and through him the Eleven) knows the Lord because he has seen him.

---

[59]Luke uses time indications to bind together the episodes in this chapter but ignores the formidable chronological difficulties in this overly long first day of the week—formidable even if for convenience Luke has ceased employing a Jewish reckoning wherein the day ends at sunset. It was already toward evening, with the day far gone (24:29), when the two disciples reclined with Jesus at table. The meal plus the long journey back on foot would make their finding the Eleven very late.

[60]This is so curious that Codex Bezae attributes the statement to the two disciples, leading to the conclusion that Simon (Peter) was the unnamed disciple alongside Cleopas on the road to Emmaus (footnote 54 above).

The Resurrection in Luke

EPISODE IN LUKE 24:36-53:
THE ELEVEN[61] GATHERED IN JERUSALEM

This episode is a literary unit in the sense that it narrates one appearance of the risen Jesus to one group in the Jerusalem area. Yet there are minor shifts of locale that suggest a subdivision: 24:36-49 takes place where the Eleven and the others are gathered together; 26:50-53 takes place as they go out to Bethany and return to the Jerusalem Temple.

(a) 24:36-49: *The appearance of Jesus at the place where the Eleven had gathered and eaten.* In 24:33 we were told that two disciples returned from Emmaus to find their colleagues gathered, but were not told where. The presence of food (24:41-42) suggests that this is a place where the Eleven had eaten. Presumably the tradition about the site of Jesus' appearance in Jerusalem was vague,[62] and Luke may have avoided imaginative specification to make it possible for his readers to relate the scene to their own house-church meetings. The greeting "Peace to you" uttered by the risen Jesus would be appropriate to that setting since it became an inter-Christian greeting.[63]

---

[61]Technically the group includes "the Eleven and those with them" (24:34). However, since "those with them" are never identified here (cf. Acts 1:14) and they play no distinct role, I shall refer simply to the Eleven throughout the episode.

[62]John 20:19, 26 has a comparable resurrection appearance take place in a site where the doors were shut. Mark 16:14 has Jesus appearing to the Eleven while they were reclining at table. Acts 2:1 sets the Pentecost scene where the Twelve (Eleven plus Matthias) were "all together in the same place." The idea that the resurrection appearances and descent of the Spirit took place in the large upper room where Jesus ate the Passover meal with his disciples (Luke 22:12-14) is a guess of later harmonization.

[63]See John 20:19, 26 and the frequent use of "Peace" in Paul's greetings to churches. This expression and other verses in this episode are omitted in Codex Bezae and some witnesses of the Western textual tradition; but today there is an increasing tendency to regard the disputed passages as authentically Lucan.

The Resurrection in Luke

At the beginning of the episode there is a strong Lucan effort to make clear that Jesus is not a spirit or a ghost but has a real body (he can eat), indeed the same body that was crucified (his hands and feet are marked in a visible way). It may well be that Luke wrote this scene with apologetic intent. He may have sought to refute non-believers who rejected the resurrection (24:39: "It really is I!") and/or to correct incipient Christian gnostics or docetists who denied that there was a bodily element to Jesus' victory over death (24:39 "No spirit/ghost has flesh and bones as you see me having"). Interestingly, in the Lucan sequence the Eleven who believe that Jesus has been raised (24:34) have doubts in their hearts (24:38) and even disbelieve (24:41)[64] when Jesus insists on his bodily reality. Others detect a more didactic goal in the passage: Christians expecting their own bodily resurrection may have sought more knowledge about it through reflection on the risen body of Jesus.

In any case Luke offers the most materially realistic view of the body of the risen Jesus found in the New Testament. Some modern scholars judge his presentation excessively naive; but that may be because they themselves do not accept the reality of the bodily resurrection, a reality on which I think all the pertinent New Testament writers would agree. Within the agreement, however, there may well have been a difference on the material properties that the New Testament writers would attribute to the risen body of Jesus. Paul's notion of a *spiritual* body to be possessed by the risen Christian (presumably based on his experience of the risen Jesus) is related to his thesis that "flesh and blood cannot inherit the

[64]Typically Lucan is the softening of the disbelief as "because of joy"; cf. the disciples' "sleeping from sorrow" in 22:45. Here Luke uses *dialogismoi* ("doubts, negative thoughts") to describe what is in the hearts of the Eleven. In the infancy narrative (2:35) Simon recognized that in the future Jesus would play a judicial role: "The negative thoughts of many hearts will be revealed."

The Resurrection in Luke

kingdom of God" (1 Cor 15:50). This seems quite different from Luke's insistence on Jesus' flesh and bones. Nevertheless, one should acknowledge that Luke's primary interest is in the identity of the risen Jesus ("It really is I"), so that having the Eleven recognize the bodily aspect of Jesus in the eating of the fish (24:42-43) is not too different from having the two disciples at Emmaus recognize Jesus in the breaking of the bread. An important part of the risen Jesus' identity is his continuity with his corporeal existence during the ministry. That Luke is not naive is illustrated by Acts 10:40-41: "God raised him on the third day and granted that he should be manifest not to all the people but to us witnesses, chosen beforehand by God, who ate and drank with him after his resurrection from the dead." Despite the earthly properties of eating and drinking attributed to the risen Jesus, Luke recognized that there were different properties since he could not be seen by all.

Having assured the Eleven of his identity, Jesus proceeds (24:44-46) to use exactly the same pedagogy with them that he used in the previous episode with the two disciples. He explains the things written about him in the Scriptures and how they show that the Messiah had to suffer and be raised from the dead.[65] In Luke's view the interpretation of the Scriptures is an essential element in understanding the passion and resurrection. In that Luke is not far from the tradition reported by Paul in 1 Cor 15:3-5 which describes as "according to the Scriptures" the death, burial, and resurrection.

The scene now turns to a commissioning, a common fea-

---

[65]What is different here is Jesus' contention that during his time with them (the public ministry) he already told them, "All the things written about me in the Law of Moses and the Prophets and the Psalms must be fulfilled." There is no such verbatim statement of Jesus recorded in Luke's Gospel; yet the claim that both the word of Jesus and the Scriptures support what occurred in the passion is very powerful.

The Resurrection in Luke

ture in the resurrection narratives (pp. 19–20, 36, 75), even if it is phrased in different terms by the various evangelists. What is unique is that Luke brings the commissioning under the same scriptural imperative as the passion and resurrection. Not only is it written that the Messiah should suffer and rise; it is written ''that in his name repentance for the forgiveness of sins be proclaimed to all nations, beginning from Jerusalem. You are witnesses of this'' (24:47-48).[66] Since the proclamation beginning from Jerusalem will be described in Acts, in the Lucan outlook the Scriptures contain already the whole of God's plan narrated in the two-volume work (Gospel, Acts), describing the work of Jesus and that of the Spirit. The emphasis that this repentance (*metanoia*) or total change of mind for forgiveness of sins will be proclaimed (verbal form related to *kerygma*) *in Jesus' name* suggests that both preaching and baptizing are envisaged as part of the commission. For instance in Acts 2:38, *metanoia* and being baptized in the name of Jesus are joined as the basic demands imposed on those who accept the preaching of Peter about Jesus.[67] Meeting these demands will lead to the gift of the Holy Spirit. Similarly in the passage we are discussing the risen Jesus follows his prediction about *metanoia* for the forgiveness of sins with a demand that the Eleven take note: ''I am sending [*apostellein*] the promise of my Father on you'' (24:49). They are to stay in Jerusalem until they are clothed with power from on high. All these themes will be picked up

[66]Luke does not indicate what biblical passages he has in mind as backing for this mission to the Gentiles. Perhaps he thinks of various prophetic passages about the Gentiles coming to know God; but those passages envision the nations coming to Jerusalem, not an Israelite mission to them. Acts 2:16-21 has Peter citing Joel 2:28-32 (3:1-5) about the outpouring of the Spirit on all flesh.

[67]See also the joining of preaching the good news (*euangelizesthai*) with baptism in the name of Jesus in Acts 8:12. There are many references in Acts to preaching, to healing, or to baptism being done in the name of Jesus.

The Resurrection in Luke

at the beginning of Acts, making clear that Jesus is speaking of the gift of the Holy Spirit. Acts 1:4-5 speaks of *the promise of the Father* in relation to baptism with the Holy Spirit; Acts 1:8 has Jesus telling the Eleven that when the Holy Spirit comes upon them, they shall be his *witnesses* from Jerusalem to the ends of the earth; Acts 2:33 refers to their "having received from the Father *the promise* of the Holy Spirit." Some of the other Gospel commissions have the disciples themselves sent; indeed that is how they became apostles (i.e., those sent). Yet in Luke the Holy Spirit is the one sent, for that Spirit empowers the apostolic mission (Acts 15:28: "It has seemed good to the Holy Spirit and to us"). In the Lucan infancy narrative the Holy Spirit coming upon Mary as the power of the Most High brought about the conception of God's Son (1:35). At the beginning of the public ministry Jesus returned in the power of the Spirit into Galilee (4:14). At the beginning of Acts the apostles will be clothed with power when the Holy Spirit comes on them (1:8).

When one looks back at what the two disciples learned from the risen Jesus on the road to Emmaus and on what the Eleven learned in Jerusalem, beyond the assurance that Jesus had conquered death and was raised bodily, there is a remarkable message that would speak meaningfully to the communities addressed by Luke in the late first century. The demand for the *metanoia* of which Jesus speaks was placed on these Christians when the good news about Jesus was proclaimed to them; and they were baptized in the name of Jesus, which was the occasion of their receiving the Holy Spirit. The Scriptures were explained to them, with the meaning of the Law and the Prophets (and the Psalms) being enlightened through what God had done in Jesus and in the church by the Spirit. These Christians gathered together, greeting one another with "Peace to you"; and through the eyes of faith they saw that Jesus was present in the breaking of the bread. In short Luke's Christian readers could have

The Resurrection in Luke

found much of their Christian life laid out for them by the risen Jesus.

(b) 24:50-53: *Leading the Eleven to Bethany, Jesus ascends to heaven; the Eleven return to the Jerusalem Temple.* The movement to Bethany (the purpose of which is not clarified by Luke) may have belonged to the preGospel tradition. (Acts, by speaking of the Mount of Olives, will clothe the site of the ascension with Old Testament echoes.) In the Gospel opening, after the priest Zechariah received an annunciation of the birth of John the Baptist from the angel Gabriel, he was unable to speak to the people and bless them as they expected (Luke 1:10, 21-22). At the end of the Gospel Jesus blesses the Eleven in a priestly manner. We see that when we compare Luke's description of Jesus in 24:50, "Having lifted up his hands, he blessed them," with the description of the saintly high priest Simon II in Sir 50:20: "He lifted up his hands over all the congregation of Israel to pronounce the blessing of the Lord with his lips."

This blessing marks the departure of Jesus as he is taken up to heaven. On the mount of the transfiguration (9:30) Moses and Elijah (two figures who in Jewish tradition were taken up bodily into heaven) appeared in glory and spoke to Jesus of his exodus. Now, like those predecessors, Jesus makes his exodus. As Jesus is taken up, he completes the journey to Jerusalem that he began shortly after the transfiguration "when the days approached for his being taken up" (9:51).[68] Sir 50:21 describes the reaction of the people to the priestly blessing of Simon II: "They bowed down in worship." Similarly Luke 24:52 describes the reaction of the

[68]Many commentators think it unusual that Luke includes an ascension scene in his resurrection account (but see Mark 16:19 which includes sitting at God's right). Yet an element in this ascension is the termination of Jesus' earthly appearances, a concept known to Paul who lists Jesus' appearance to him as the last of all (1 Cor 15:8). Luke is giving Old Testament coloring to the idea of a final appearance that existed before the Gospels were written.

The Resurrection in Luke

Eleven to Jesus' blessing and ascension: "They worshiped him."

Then with great joy they return to Jerusalem where they are constantly in the Temple. This matches the promise of joy given to Zechariah in that Temple at the beginning of the Gospel (1:14). The last Greek words in the Gospel tell us what the Eleven do in the Temple: They bless God. No Gospel ends its account of the good news on a more beautiful note or on one that is more challenging for the Christians of all times as they come together in their own communities.

EPISODE IN ACTS 1:1-12: JESUS' PARTING
INSTRUCTIONS TO HIS APOSTLES; ASCENT TO HEAVEN
At the beginning of Acts, Luke takes pains to relate his second volume to his first,[69] which, he says, ended on the day Jesus was taken up after he had instructed his apostles through the Holy Spirit. In Acts 1:9 Luke will tell us again that Jesus was taken up to heaven; and such duplication has puzzled scholars even to the point of their postulating that another hand added one of the two accounts. Rather, Luke is using the resurrection appearances and the ascension as what I have called a hinge. From the stance of the Gospel the resurrection-ascension terminates visibly all that Jesus began to do and teach (Acts 1:1); from the stance of Acts it will prepare the apostles to be witnesses for Jesus to the ends of the earth (1:8). His using the ascension twice shows once more that despite the concreteness of his descriptions Luke has no naive understanding of what he is describing. The going of Jesus to God after death is timeless from the viewpoint of God; but there is a sequence from the viewpoint of those whose lives it touched.

In the opening description in Acts (1:1-2) two minor features are noteworthy, for they strengthen the connection be-

[69]Since I am concerned only with the resurrection features of this narrative, I leave aside the issue of the identity of Theophilus.

The Resurrection in Luke

tween Luke's two volumes. First, there is a reference to the first volume (the Gospel) as describing what Jesus *began* to do and teach. If the verb is meant literally, Luke sees Jesus as continuing spiritually his activity in Acts, even though he has ascended into heaven. Second, Jesus is said to have instructed his chosen apostles through the Holy Spirit before he was taken up (in the first volume). Thus while Luke will describe the coming of the Holy Spirit in Acts 2, he recognizes that the Spirit was already active in Jesus' interpretation of Scripture and commissioning of the apostles as described in Luke 24.

On the other hand, Acts 1:3 tells us something we would never have expected from the Gospel, namely, that for forty days after his passion and death Jesus made appearances to his apostles. The reference to Jesus giving "many proofs" showing that he was alive and speaking to the apostles of the kingdom of God suggests that Luke is thinking of the type of appearance narrated in the episode we have just considered (24:36-49), where Jesus showed his hands and feet and ate fish to prove that it was he and not a ghost, and where he instructed the Eleven about the Scriptures and the future preaching of *metanoia*. In making the apostles the recipients of more than one appearance Luke may be reflecting an early tradition similar to that in 1 Cor 15:5-8 where among the six persons or groups to whom Jesus appeared are listed Cephas (Peter), the Twelve, and Paul.[70] As I pointed out in footnote 68, such traditions set a time limit after which Jesus did not appear, although the limit Paul cites is considerably longer than either of the two Lucan limits ("the same day" in Luke 24; forty days in Acts). The role of the forty days becomes clear when we reflect on

[70]Despite the claim of some scholars that Luke considered only the Twelve apostles, he calls Paul an apostle in Acts 14:14. It is not clear whether Luke would extend the term to others mentioned in the 1 Corinthians list, e.g., James the brother of the Lord and "all the apostles [beyond the Twelve]."

The Resurrection in Luke

Luke's predilection for architectonic arrangement, noted at the beginning of this chapter. In Luke 4:1-2 Jesus was led by the Spirit to spend forty days in the desert, after which he returned in the power of the Spirit to begin his ministry in Galilee (4:14). By way of balance it is appropriate that Acts too begins with a forty-day preparatory period. In both instances Luke is evoking the forty years in the desert during which God prepared Israel for entrance into the Promised Land. This imagery fits well with the way in which the beginning of Acts symbolically associates the beginnings of the Christian community with the beginnings of Israel, e.g., the completion of the number twelve (Acts 1:15-26) so that the Christian parallel to the twelve Israelite patriarchs may be made perfect; also the Sinai symbolism in the description of the Pentecost event (wind, fire, Pentecost as the feast of the giving of the Law to Israel). The God who called Israel so long before to be His covenanted people is following the same patterns in His renewal of the covenant through Jesus Christ.

Moving on from his general introduction in Acts 1:1-3, Luke proceeds to describe appearances in which Jesus addresses himself directly to his apostles. In the first (1:4-5)[71] Jesus calls attention to the fact that the message he gives them (not to distance themselves from Jerusalem but to wait for the promise of the Father) is one that they already heard from him (see Luke 24:49). Yet here he makes the clarifying addition that the promise of the Father is to be fulfilled when they are baptized in the Holy Spirit not many days from now. Thus the risen Jesus reminds his apostles not only of

[71]The context supplied by 1:4 depends on the translation given to *synalizomenos*, whether it means "being assembled with," or "dwelling with," or "eating with." If the last, we have another instance of the meal setting that is common in resurrection appearances. If the first, we have another vaguely described meeting of the Eleven/Twelve, similar to the one that will follow in 1:6 (also Luke 24:33).

The Resurrection in Luke

what *he* said when he appeared to them at Easter but of
what John the Baptist said at the beginning of the ministry
when he contrasted his own baptizing with water and the
coming baptism in the Holy Spirit and fire (Luke 3:16).[72]
From the beginning to the end of his first volume, Luke prepared for the coming of the Spirit that would mark the second volume.

In another appearance (Acts 1:6-8) Jesus goes beyond
reminders to supply an important revelation. Both during the
public ministry and after the resurrection Jesus spoke of the
kingdom of God (Luke 4:43; Acts 1:3); and now his disciples,
gathered together, ask about that kingdom which they understand as a kingdom to be restored to Israel. Their understanding is not illogical: the raising of Jesus showed that God
had definitively intervened in history and that Jesus is the
Messiah (Luke 24:26), i.e., the anointed king of the House of
David who was expected to reestablish the Davidic kingdom.
Thus in their question the apostles are vocalizing an understanding that would have been shared by many who heard
(of) Jesus of Nazareth. Scholars debate endlessly about Jesus'
own view of the kingdom of God. The differing views in the
New Testament are explained more easily if Jesus was never
lucidly specific about the extent to which the kingdom would
be visible and/or invisible, about whether it would come soon
(in this generation) or in the less definite future, about
whether it would exist in this world and/or in the next.[73] Be
that as it may, here Luke presents that side of Jesus' teaching that makes sense of the two-volume Lucan work and of

[72]Acts 1:5 does not repeat the "in fire" phrase of the Baptist, but the
Pentecost baptism of the apostles in the Holy Spirit will be accompanied by
"tongues as of fire" (Acts 2:3).

[73]Although divine, Jesus was truly human; and so many wonder whether
he had exact knowledge of such things. They point to a saying of Jesus
which has parallels to his statement here but which Mark 13:32 places in the
public ministry: "Of that day or that hour no one knows, not even the angels in heaven, nor the Son, but only the Father."

The Resurrection in Luke

the world-wide missionary thrust so prominent in the second volume. If the risen Jesus were going to bring about the kingdom immediately as part of the end of the world, there would be no point to writing books for future readers,[74] or to embarking on a mission that would not have time to reach the ends of the earth. The firm answer that Luke reports from the risen Jesus, "It is not for you to know the times or the seasons that the Father has set by His own authority," defuses chronological speculation about God's final intervention, and has been reiterated by the church at large ever since as a response to sectarians in each generation who spend time and religious energy calculating the time of the second coming. It is much more important that Jesus' followers, empowered by the Holy Spirit, spend their time and energy bearing witness to him.

Luke uses Jesus' emphasis on witness to present (Acts 1:8) the outline of this second volume that he is writing. Acts 2-7 will concern the witness borne in Jerusalem culminating in Stephen's witness by his blood. Acts 8-12 will concern events of a decisive nature occurring chiefly in Samaria and Judea, culminating with both Peter and Paul leaving Jerusalem for more distant places.[75] Acts 13–28 will concern the great mis-

[74]It is not accidental that the first Christian writing (before 70) consists of letters addressed to the immediate present, and that only about 70 and the fall of Jerusalem do we get a more permanent literature that may envision future readers.

[75]Others would apply the "Judea and Samaria" section of Jesus' words to Acts 8-10, regarding chapter 10 as the terminus since there a Gentile is converted. Yet the action in chapters 11-12 is largely in Judea. That Luke has fashioned Jesus' words from his own plan for the book becomes apparent when we realize that, although the apostles are supposed to have received this directive at the beginning, the spread of Christianity to the Samaritans and the Gentiles utterly astounds some when it takes place, and there are debates about whether this is justified. Moreover, although the apostles are told to be the witnesses who follow this itinerary, the Twelve (except Peter and John) largely remain in Jerusalem, and others are responsible for the spreading witness.

The Resurrection in Luke

sion to the Gentiles starting out from Antioch and ending in Rome, and thus to the ends of the earth.[76]

Having thus prepared his apostles in detail for the future, Jesus is taken up to heaven (Acts 1:9). Here Luke is even more graphic than in 24:51, for this time a cloud intervenes to take him from their sight. (This is similar to the cloud of divine presence mentioned by Luke 9:34-35 at the transfiguration.) Two men in white suddenly are standing there to interpret the event for Jesus' followers, even as two (angelic) men in dazzling apparel were standing by the empty tomb to interpret that for the women (24:4-7). Their interpretation of the ascension gains eschatological coloring from information that Luke supplies as the episode ends in Acts 1:12, namely, that this ascension takes place on the Mount called Olivet.[77] The most prominent scriptural reference to the Mount of Olives comes at the end of the prophetic collection, in Zech 14:4-21 where we are told that God will come there with his holy ones to exercise the great judgment and to manifest his kingship over all the earth. No wonder then that at this place the two men can give the assurance that Jesus, taken up this way, "will come (back) in the same way as you saw him going" (Acts 1:11). The cloud that takes Jesus from their sight is related to that coming, for Luke 21:27 promised that "they will see the Son of Man coming in a cloud with power and great glory."

It is interesting how the revelation given by the Lucan angels pertains to our times. Many liberal Christians, confusing the simple biblical description with the deeper underlying

[76]The *Psalms of Solomon* 8:15 associates Rome with "the ends of earth."

[77]Presumably, then, the gathering of the disciples in Acts 1:6, to whom Jesus speaks, also takes place on the Mount, for we are not told that they went out to this site—contrast Luke 24:50: "Jesus led them out as far as Bethany." Clearly there was a tradition about Jesus' departure for heaven from this area east of Jerusalem, but Acts plays on its theological possibilities.

The Resurrection in Luke

reality, reject the second coming as simplistic; often this leads them to think that by good endeavor and social justice they will build the kingdom in this world. Luke's narratives of the appearances of the risen Jesus insist that it really is God's kingdom; only He can establish it and He will do that through His Son. By ignoring God's authority human endeavor, no matter how religiously benevolent, will build another Tower of Babel rather than the kingdom. On the other hand, those who believe in God's activity and spend their time looking up to heaven for the second coming, as if they could calculate it, are really also rejecting God's authority in which only He knows the times and the seasons. The ironic question of the two heavenly speakers, "Men of Galilee, why do you stand peering into heaven?" (Acts 1:11), constitutes advice that there is little danger of missing the second coming (no matter what it consists in). Therefore it makes little sense to seek to gain mastery of the times and seasons as if God could be controlled. Matthew ends his account of the resurrection with the assurance that Jesus is with us all days till the end of time; Luke, who twice describes Jesus' departure, ends the resurrection story with the assurance that he will come back just as surely as he left. Meanwhile, there is the promise of the Father, the Holy Spirit.

The Resurrection in Luke

Chapter 4

The Resurrection in John 20
—A Series of Diverse Reactions

John is a Gospel of encounters: Nicodemus, the Samaritan woman at the well, the cripple at Bethesda, the man born blind, Mary and Martha, and even Pilate. One after the other they have made their entrance onto the Johannine stage to encounter Jesus, the light come into the world; and in so doing they have judged themselves by whether or not they continue to come to the light or turn away and prefer darkness (John 3:19-21). It is not surprising, then, that the principal Johannine account of the appearances of the risen Jesus becomes a series of encounters illustrating different faith reactions.

The following arrangement of four episodes can be observed:

(1) 20:1-10: Reactions of Simon Peter and the Beloved Disciple
(2) 20:11-18: Reaction of Mary Magdalene
(3) 20:19-23: Reaction of Disciples
(4) 20:24-29: Reaction of Thomas

The first pair of episodes takes place in relation to the tomb, early on Easter Sunday morning; the second pair of episodes takes place where the disciples are gathered, first on Easter Sunday evening and then a week later. Although the respective characters in the episodes are interrelated, the reaction of one does not influence the reaction of the other. The total scenario reminds us that in the range of belief there are different degrees of readiness and different factors that cause people to come to faith.

In all four Gospels women come to the empty tomb on the
first day of the week, but only in John does Mary Magdalene
visit the tomb twice. The second visit (John 20:11ff.) is the
one that has major parallels to the other Gospel accounts; the
first visit functions mostly to set the stage for the story of
Simon Peter and the Beloved Disciple. Even in such a stage
setting, however, there are Johannine touches. As in Mark
and Luke, Mary Magdalene[78] comes "early," but only in
John do we have the added indication that "it was still
dark." In this Gospel where light and darkness play such a
role, darkness lasts until someone believes in the risen Jesus.
We are not told why Magdalene comes to the tomb;[79] but her
alarmed reaction of racing off to tell the two disciples, "They
took the Lord from the tomb, and we do not know where
they put him!" (the first of the three times she stresses this),
suggests a personal attachment to Jesus—an attachment the
Good Shepherd will draw on later in the scene. Her immediate conclusion that Jesus' body has been stolen, a conclusion
reached seemingly without entering the tomb, is peculiar to
John. Matthew 28:13-15 attributes to "the Jews" the calumny
that Jesus' disciples stole the body; but Mary Magdalene
jumps to the conclusion that Jesus' "enemies" have done
this, for she reports to *disciples* that others have stolen the
body. Later (20:19) we shall hear of doors being closed "for
fear of the Jews." This has been a Gospel shaped by an-

[78]That Mary Magdalene was not alone is suggested by her "we" in 20:2.
However, since she is the sole recipient of the appearance of Jesus in 20:11-18
(and in that John may be closer to original tradition than Matt 28:9-10 where
"the other Mary" also sees the risen Jesus), any others who went to the
tomb with Magdalene tend to fade into the background in John's understanding of the tradition. John is fascinated by the dramatic possibilities of
individuals, even if a group is present.

[79]In Mark and Luke she comes to anoint the body; in Matthew, to see the
sepulcher guarded by soldiers.

The Resurrection in John 20

tagonism between the followers of Jesus and the synagogue, and that hostile context carries over to the resurrection account.

The two disciples who respond to Magdalene's report about the tomb are Simon Peter and the Beloved Disciple. The latter figure, never mentioned as such during the first part of the Gospel which describes Jesus' public ministry, has appeared with startling frequency in the second part when "the hour has come for Jesus to pass from this world to the Father" (13:1). He belongs to that context where "having loved his own who were in the world, Jesus loved them to the end." Before John 20 this disciple has appeared at the Last Supper next to Jesus, in the high priest's courtyard next to Simon Peter, and near the cross of Jesus next to Jesus' mother. These contexts have been recounted in detail by the Synoptic evangelists who, however, never seem to have seen the presence of this disciple; for them he is the invisible man. The present instance is no exception: Luke 24:12 tells us that Peter arose and ran to the tomb, looked in, saw the linen cloths, and went home wondering.[80] Luke gives no indication of the companion disciple who features so prominently in John. Yet Luke 24:24 may give us a key to this enigma: "Some of those who were with us went to the tomb and found it just as the women said." In other words Luke knows of several disciples going to the tomb, and yet is capable earlier of mentioning only Peter because the others were not important as witnesses. The one whom John calls the disciple whom Jesus loved may have been invisible to the Synoptic tradition because he had no great name or rank, whereas his presence was eminently memorable to others who had a different criterion of greatness. For them he had

[80]This verse in Luke is textually dubious. Some scholars theorize that it was added by a later scribe who copied it from John; others suggest that it was originally part of Luke but excised by a scribe, because, by not mentioning the Beloved Disciple, it seemingly contradicted John. See footnote 49.

The Resurrection in John 20

the highest rank of all because Jesus loved him. John 20:2 uses two titles: The first is "the other disciple"; the second is "the disciple whom Jesus loved." The first may have been the way he was evaluated (and therefore forgotten) by other Christians; the second was the way he was known to those who preserved his memory in the Johannine tradition.

John paints artistically the delicate relationship between this disciple and the famous Peter (with whom he has appeared in a situation involving contrast twice before [13:23-24; 18:15-16] and will appear twice more [21:7, 20-22]). That the disciple reached the tomb first but did not enter, allowing Peter to catch up and enter first, has been the subject of imaginative speculation as to who had the greater ecclesiastical dignity. In fact, the arrangement may be dramatic, not theological: his entering last makes the disciple's reaction the culmination of the episode. In any case, neither the arrival nor the entry is the featured point of John's contrast between the two figures. What matters to the evangelist is that they responded differently to what they saw in the tomb, namely, the burial garments and the separate headpiece without the body: The disciple believed, and nothing is said to indicate that Peter believed.[81] In the Pauline list of those to whom the risen Jesus appeared, the name of Cephas (Peter) comes before all others (1 Cor 15:5). But John knows of one who believed in the risen Lord even before an appearance, with a perspicacity that arose from love.

John 20:8 relates this belief to what the disciple saw, namely, the burial garments in an otherwise empty tomb. Be-

---

[81]I am not impressed by the argument that if John meant that Peter did not believe, he would have mentioned it. John does nothing to denigrate Simon Peter who in his estimation was one of Jesus' "own" whom he loved to the very end (13:1, 36), and who stayed with Jesus when others turned away because he recognized in Jesus the Holy One of God who had the words of eternal life (6:66-69). What John wishes to *emphasize* here is not the failure of Simon Peter to believe but the extraordinary sensitivity of the other disciple, stemming from the love of Jesus, that enables him to believe.

The Resurrection in John 20

cause the evangelist takes such care to describe the burial wrappings lying there, with the piece of cloth that covered the head rolled up in a place by itself, many have thought that the configuration of these garments was significant to the disciple, e.g., that they preserved the form of Jesus' body. Others have contended that the presence of the garments caused the disciple to deduce that the body had not been stolen, for grave robbers would scarcely have taken the time to unwrap the corpse and carry it away naked. Such reasoning does not explain why neither Simon Peter nor Mary Magdalene were moved to faith from having seen the garments. A better suggestion involves inner Johannine symbolism. Lazarus came forth from the tomb "bound hand and foot with linen strips and his face wrapped in a cloth" (John 11:44); Jesus has left the same twofold set of wrappings in the tomb. Lazarus was resuscitated to natural life but would die again and need his burial garments once more. By contrast, the garments left in Jesus' tomb revealed to the disciple that Jesus had been raised to eternal life. The added Johannine comment that "as yet they did not understand the Scripture that Jesus had to rise from the dead" explains Simon Peter's failure to understand, for, as Luke 24:25-27, 32 shows, explanation of the Scriptures helped Jesus' disciples to accept the resurrection. Once more, by contrast, the extraordinary sensitivity of the first one to believe after the resurrection is highlighted since this disciple needed no such help.

EPISODE IN 20:11-18: REACTION OF MARY MAGDALENE
In 20:10 we read: "With this the disciples went back home." The evangelist's dramatic preference for individual encounter with Jesus has led him carefully to remove Simon Peter and the Beloved Disciple from the tomb before the episode in which Mary Magdalene comes to faith there. The faith perception by the disciple and Simon Peter's lack of it have no

The Resurrection in John 20

influence on Magdalene whose reaction must be evaluated on its own. Next to Peter, James, John, and Judas, we note that Magdalene is the most frequently mentioned Gospel follower of Jesus (fourteen times in all) and as such is a worthy character for the Johannine stage. In describing Mary's second visit to the tomb, John rejoins the common Christian tradition that she encountered an angelic presence there. Peculiar to John is the artistic touch that carefully positions one angel at the head and the other at the foot of the place where Jesus had lain—a positioning comparable to the careful description in 20:6-7 that positioned separately the burial wrappings and the cloth that had covered Jesus' head. Readers are not meant to ask why these angels were not there when Simon Peter and the Beloved Disciple entered the tomb. John is illustrating different reactions as greater aids to faith are supplied. In the previous episode Magdalene's first impression at the tomb was negative (20:1-2: "They took the Lord from the tomb, and we do not know where they put him"), but it served as a transition to the positive main story of how the Beloved Disciple came to faith (20:3-10). Similarly here, despite the presence of the angels, Magdalene's second impression at the tomb is negative (20:11-13: "They took my Lord away, and I do not know where they put him"), but it serves as a transition to the positive main story where she will come to faith (20:14-18). That development is made possible, not by angels but by Jesus himself.

The appearance to Magdalene may have been a very old tradition, despite the absence of women's names from a more official list of witnesses to the resurrection in 1 Cor 15:5ff.[82] John has expanded the traditional material into a dramatic encounter. Even though Jesus stands plainly in sight and speaks to Magdalene, she does not recognize him. Jesus' question "Whom [*tina*] are you looking for?" echoes the first

[82]I discussed this in relation to Matt 28:9-10 on pp. 30-31 above.

The Resurrection in John 20

words he spoke in this Gospel, for in 1:38, when Jesus turned around and saw two disciples of John the Baptist following, he asked, "What [ti] are you looking for?" It is a question that probes discipleship,[83] voiced most recently and tragically (18:4) in the garden across the Kidron to the arresting party brought by Judas to seize Jesus. The disciples of John the Baptist stayed with Jesus and found the Messiah (1:41). The arresting party was hostilely looking for Jesus the Nazorean; they found him but were struck down in judgment (18:6). Magdalene is looking for the dead Jesus; she will find the living Lord.

Although the failure to recognize Jesus is a common feature in Gospel resurrection narratives, the way John dramatizes Magdalene's lack of recognition is unique. Her reiterated supposition that people have carried Jesus off and her consuming concern to know where they have put him now fasten in on one whom she supposes to be the gardener (20:15), that is, the caretaker of the garden in which John 19:41 (alone) has told us Jesus was buried. The depth of Mary's concern can be seen in the question posed to her both by the angels and by the unrecognized Jesus: "Why are you weeping?", a query that gives the impression that tears have blurred her vision to heavenly interventions. The failure to see is overcome only when Jesus calls her by name. In John 10:3, 5 the Good (or really, Model) Shepherd was said to call by name the sheep that belong to him, sheep who will not follow a stranger "because they do not recognize the voice of strangers." Mary's spontaneous reaction to being called by name, namely her addressing Jesus as "Rabbuni,"

[83]The parallelism constituted by a similar question in the opening and closing Gospel scenes takes for granted that both men and women are disciples of Jesus in John—something not necessarily true elsewhere, for in Matthew "disciples" seem to be equated with the Twelve. Discipleship is the only category that is given importance in John, and it is open equally to all who believe and are begotten as children by God.

The Resurrection in John 20

an endearing term for Teacher, verifies that claim of the Good Shepherd. In the instance of the Beloved Disciple, a faith that stemmed from seeing the now-useless burial clothes represented one form of perceptiveness based on love. A faith that stems from Mary's hearing her name called represents another form: She is one of those of whom Jesus said: "I know my sheep and mine know me" (10:14).

Admixed in Magdalene's recognition and the love it reflects is an all too human element or, as John would phrase it, an element of this world below. Matthew's account (28:9) of the appearance to the women at the tomb has them clutching Jesus' feet. Something like that may be supposed here, for Jesus tells Mary, "Do not cling to me." She would hold on to his presence, keeping him here below; but he must remind her of the import of both clauses in the evaluation of his followers that he gave at the Last Supper (John 17:14): "They do not belong to the world any more than I belong to the world." When Jesus says to Magdalene, "I am ascending to my Father," he is reiterating where his home is, namely, the world above to which he belongs. When he adds "and to your Father," he is revealing to her that because of her post-resurrectional faith the world to which she now belongs is also above—the heavenly house of Jesus' Father in which there are prepared many mansions (14:2). In indicating that "my Father" is now "your Father,"[84] Jesus is vocalizing in his own words the promise of the Prologue (1:12): "All those who did accept him he empowered to become God's children." That same new status is reflected in Jesus' reference to the disciples as "my brothers" in 20:17 as he sends Mary out to proclaim to them his ascension.[85] If at the beginning of

[84]The pattern is found in Ruth 1:16: Urged by Naomi to stay behind in Moab, Ruth insists that, though not an Israelite, she will come to Israel with Naomi; for from this moment, "Your people shall be my people, and your God my God."

[85]On the general use of "brothers" for the disciples, see p. 31

The Resurrection in John 20

the tomb story, Mary Magdalene (named in full only at the beginning and the end: 20:1 and 18) went to tell the disciples that "They took the Lord from the tomb," at the end of the tomb story she goes to tell them, "I have seen the Lord." She already knew that he was Lord from what he had done in his lifetime, but now she understands the profundity of that title from what he has revealed after his resurrection. He is now more than the "Rabbuni" whom she lovingly recognized when he first called her name. The Beloved Disciple was the first to believe; Magdalene is the first to proclaim *the risen Lord.*[86]

EPISODE IN 20:19-23: REACTION OF THE DISCIPLES
In narrating Jesus' appearance to the group of disciples (as already in the instance of Magdalene's [second] visit to the tomb), John is close to common tradition, for several Gospels describe a commissioning appearance of Jesus to the Twelve or Eleven.[87] Once more, however, John has his own way of

above. The Beloved Disciple already became Jesus' brother at the cross in John 19:26-27 when Jesus said to his mother in reference to the disciple, "Woman, here is your son." We shall see other instances of the priority of the Beloved Disciple in gifts and experiences that ultimately come to the rest of those who believe in Jesus.

[86]In chapter 21 we shall see that although the Beloved Disciple has a certain priority over Simon Peter in faith and love, he is not made a shepherd of the sheep. Here in chapter 20 his priority in faith does not make him a proclaimer of resurrection faith. The relation of the disciple to Jesus is interior; exteriorly his only service is to witness (19:35). As for Magdalene, while her proclamation of the risen Lord is (in the language of other New Testament works) an apostolic role, we should remember that "apostle" is not Johannine terminology.

[87]See Luke 24:36-49; Mark 16:14-18; Matt 28:16-20; also 1 Cor 15:5. John does not define which "disciples" were present; but the absence of Thomas, "one of the Twelve" (John 20:24), suggests that others of the Twelve were among the disciples. John does not demote the Twelve (see 6:67-69 where they have a special attachment to Jesus), but his use of "disciples" is more widely representative of those who would believe in Jesus. If one puts together 20:2,

The Resurrection in John 20

arranging the reactions. In 20:1 he gave this setting: "Early on the first day of the week when it was still dark"; in 20:19 he gives this setting: "On the evening of that first day of the week when, for fear of the Jews, the disciples had locked the doors of the place where they were." The darkness has been dispelled since the Beloved Disciple and Mary Magdalene know that the Lord is risen; but fear and hiding still mark the lives of the disciples, despite Magdalene's report to them of what had happened at the tomb. Yet the fact that the disciples have already heard that Magdalene has seen the Lord makes intelligible the absence of doubt when they see Jesus appear.

His "Peace to you" (a statement of fact, not a wish) in 20:19 goes beyond a greeting[88] because of what Jesus proclaimed at the Last Supper: " 'Peace' is my farewell to you; my 'peace' is my gift to you; and I do not give it to you as the world gives it"—words Jesus coupled with the statement that if he was going away, he was also "coming back to you" (14:27-28). Next, in 20:20, the risen Jesus shows his disciples his hands and side, with the wound-marks inflicted during the crucifixion (as 20:25 will make clear). He thus removes all question of his identity[89] and fulfills a Last Supper

10, and 18, one might judge that the disciple whom Jesus loved should be present; but one can never anticipate the reappearance of that mysterious figure.

[88]While "Peace to . . ." is a general greeting in rabbinic Hebrew, in biblical Hebrew the *shalom* greeting tends to be confined to solemn, often revelatory moments, e.g., Judg 6:23.

[89]In Luke 24:37-40 the invitation "See my hands and feet" responds explicitly to questionings that rise in the heart of the disciples who think they are seeing a spirit. While Jesus' showing his hands and side in John 20:20 and inviting Thomas to examine his wounds in 20:27 imply a certain tangible corporality, the fact that Jesus comes and appears in front of the disciples even though the doors are locked (20:19) should make us wary of assuming that John had a crassly physical understanding of the body of the risen Jesus. There is no solid Gospel evidence that the appearance of the risen Jesus to his disciples on earth was other than bodily (and certainly no

The Resurrection in John 20

promise (16:21-22): "You are sad now; but I shall see you again, and your hearts will rejoice with a joy that no one can take from you." In reporting the reaction of the disciples John says that they saw that it was "the Lord," and this use of the standard postresurrectional title is the closest that John comes to telling us that they believed. Their insight brings them joy, a response that fulfills the goal enunciated by Jesus at the Last Supper (16:24): ". . . in order that your joy may be full."

Jesus repeats "Peace to you" (20:21); this not only further clarifies that we have here no simple greeting, but also suggests that peace is to accompany the disciples in their forthcoming assignments. The first of those is conveyed through a commissioning: "As the Father has sent me [*apostellein*], so do I send you [*pempein*]." While John's stylistic preference for varied vocabulary plays a major role in such an alternation of the verbs "to send," the fact that he does not use the title "apostle" (*apostolos*) may explain why here he does not repeat *apostellein* in reference to the disciples. Nevertheless, this is a commissioning comparable in large part to the apostolic commissioning of the Twelve (Eleven) in Luke 24:46-49; Matthew 28:18-19; and Mark 16:15.⁹⁰ The paradigm for the commissioning in John is the Father's sending of Jesus with all that implies by way of purpose, e.g., to bring life, light, truth. Just as the Father was present in the Son during the Son's mission (12:45: "Whoever sees me is seeing him who sent me"), so now must the disciples in their mission manifest the presence of Jesus to the point that whoever sees the disciples sees Jesus who sent them. That is an enor-

evidence that his body remained in the grave); yet there is much evidence that this was a different kind of body or one with different properties from the body before death.

⁹⁰I say "in large part" because the other commissionings specify the destination (the world, the Gentiles); in John 20:21 the mission is as wide as that of Jesus' mission from the Father.

mous challenge! It was anticipated at the Last Supper (13:20): "Whoever welcomes anyone that I shall send welcomes me, and whoever welcomes me welcomes him who sent me."

Such re-presenting of Jesus on the part of the disciples becomes possible through the gift of the Holy Spirit (20:22). Jesus was designated by John the Baptist as "The one who is to baptize with the Holy Spirit" (1:33);[91] and at the Last Supper he promised to send the Holy Spirit (15:26). That promise is now fulfilled for the disciples when the risen Jesus says to them, "Receive the Holy Spirit."[92] A particular aspect of this gift of the Spirit is signaled by Jesus' breathing on the disciples, a gesture that even in vocabulary is evocative of Genesis 2:7: "The Lord God formed the human being out of the dust of the earth and breathed into his nostrils the breath of life." We should be aware that "spirit, wind, breath" often represent the same vocabulary cluster, for that makes intelligible the passionate exclamation of Ezek 37:9: "From the four winds come, O spirit, and breathe into these slain that they may come to life." This motif is repeated close to New Testament times by Wis 15:11: "The One who fashioned [the human being] and breathed into him a living spirit." Just as in the first creation God's breath brought into existence a human being in his image and likeness, so now Jesus' gift of his own Holy Spirit makes the disciples God's children in the likeness of the Son. Now they are born of Spirit (John

[91]The gift of the Holy Spirit in 20:22 is connected in the next verse with the forgiveness of sins; notice that before John the Baptist's description of Jesus cited above, he described him as "the Lamb of God who takes away the sin of the world" (1:29).

[92]At Jesus' death his Spirit was given over to the Beloved Disciple and to the mother of Jesus (who had now become the mother of the disciple) as they stood near the cross (John 19:26-27). Notice that in many aspects of the complex of resurrection/ascension/gift-of-the-Spirit the Beloved Disciple has priority over the other disciples in John. Different New Testament works will deal with that complex in different ways, e.g., Acts 2 has still another moment for the giving of the Spirit (Pentecost).

The Resurrection in John 20

3:5). The breath of God in Genesis gave life; the breath of Jesus gives eternal life.

In addition John relates Jesus' gift of the Spirit to the power over sin: "If you forgive people's sins, their sins are forgiven; if you hold them, they are held fast." Jesus was sent as the Lamb of God to take away the sin of the world (John 1:29; see also 1 John 2:1-2); he now shares that power with his disciples. The description of this power as including both forgiveness and binding is related to the fact that the coming of Jesus produces a *krisis* or judgment as to whether people will opt for darkness or light, so that some are condemned and some are not (John 3:18-21). If Jesus so mirrored God that when people met him they were forced to self-judgment, his disciples must so mirror Jesus that those who encounter them are provoked to a similar *krisis*. At the Last Supper (17:18) Jesus spoke more specifically than here of sending his disciples *into the world*; in that context he spoke both of the world hating them (17:14) and of the world believing because of them (17:21). The provoking of *krisis* or self-judgment is not the total range of the forgiveness and binding of sin granted in John 20:23,[93] but it is an aspect that John would not have us overlook. To represent Christ to a degree that forces people to make a decision in their lives is a tremendous empowerment.

EPISODE IN 20:24-29: REACTION OF THOMAS

In a transitional verse (20:24) John tells the reader that Thomas the Twin[94] was absent. He has been portrayed in

---

[93]Patristic writers will see the power over sin granted in John 20:23 as being exercised in baptism; later writers and the Council of Trent will see it applied in the sacrament of penance and will specify that this exercise of the power is not granted to all Christians. As legitimate as these specifications are, there is no requirement to think that the evangelist had them in mind. Our concern here is to understand this power in light of the overall Gospel context dealing with sin and judgment.

[94]It is not clear why the evangelist takes the trouble to explain the meaning

The Resurrection in John 20

John 11:16 and 14:5 as a figure not easily persuaded. The disciples who saw the risen Jesus in 20:19-23 give to Thomas exactly the same report that Mary Magdalene had given to them (20:18): "We have seen the Lord." On the basis of Magdalene's report the disciples did not doubt when Jesus appeared to them; but Thomas is adamant in his refusal to believe on the basis of their word. He wants to probe the wounds of Jesus in order to be sure. Other evangelists mention doubt on the part of the disciples after the resurrection (Matt 28:17; Luke 24:11, 41; Mark 16:11, 14); only John dramatizes that doubt so personally in an individual. Thomas' words, "If I do not see . . . and put my finger . . ., I shall never believe," reflect an attitude condemned by Jesus in John 4:48: "Unless you people can see signs and wonders you never believe." The Jesus of John does not reject the possibility that miracles lead people to faith, but he does reject miracles demanded as an absolute condition.

That "after eight days" Jesus appears in the same place (once more with the doors locked) may indicate that there was already a reverence for Sundays in the Johannine community. (Indeed in the same decade of the 90s in which the Gospel of John was written we find a reference to "the Lord's Day" in Revelation 1:10.[95]) There is a touch of Johannine irony in having the time and circumstances of the appearance to the disciples the same as those of the appearance to Thomas. Jesus' "Peace to you" is repeated despite

of the Semitic form underlying "Thomas." Some have speculated that he was Jesus' twin in appearance; in gnostic speculation he becomes the recipient of special revelations.

[95]It is not unlikely, even if unprovable, that the eucharist would have been celebrated on a Sunday thus designated, and that would mean the presence of the risen Lord. Less certain is the interpretation of "after eight days" as the first evidence of a Christian theology of the eighth day (*ogdoad*), illustrated later in the *Epistle of Barnabas* 15:9: "We celebrate with gladness the eighth day in which Jesus also rose from the dead, and having appeared, ascended into heaven."

The Resurrection in John 20

Thomas' antecedent doubts! Knowing what Thomas has said (even as he had shown previous knowledge of what was in the human heart [2:25]), Jesus invites Thomas to examine his hands and side—an invitation that turns the tables on Thomas by probing him. Scholars have debated whether in fact Thomas physically probed the risen body. Surely, on the basis of Johannine theology, however, if Thomas had examined and touched Jesus' body, he would have persisted in a disbelief that he had already demonstrated and would have ceased to be a disciple. The words of Jesus as he challenges Thomas should be taken literally: "Do not persist in your disbelief, but become a believer." Thomas accepts that directive, does not touch Jesus, and so professes faith.

The final irony of the Gospel is that the disciple who doubted the most gives expression to the highest evaluation of Jesus uttered in any gospel: "My Lord and my God." At the beginning of the Gospel the evangelist told the readers that the Word was God (1:1). Now by an inclusion he has shown how difficult it was for Jesus' followers to come to such an insight. Thomas has been remembered in Christian imagery as the doubter par excellence; yet the last words of Jesus to him in response to his confession of faith are an enviable encomium, "You have believed."

If the Gospel narrative ended at that point, we would have been satisfied that in chapter 20 we had seen four different reactions to the risen Jesus. Much to our surprise Jesus and the evangelist are interested in a fifth reaction. The Beloved Disciple believed when he saw the garments left in the tomb; Mary Magdalene believed when she heard the voice of the risen Jesus call her name; the disciples believed when they saw the risen Jesus and realized that it was the Lord; Thomas believed when challenged by the risen Jesus to carry out a disbelieving program of probing. The final praise for belief, however, is extended by Jesus to those who have believed without seeing garments or bodily presence. In the

Johannine portrait no greater praise can be given to Jesus than "My Lord and my God"; no greater praise can be given to Jesus' followers than "Blessed are those who have not seen and yet have believed." Through that faith the prophecy of Hos 2:25 (23) is fulfilled: A people that was formerly not a people has said, "You are my God." Or, in the words the evangelist uses to describe the purpose of his Gospel, through that faith the followers of Jesus "have life in his name" (John 20:31).

The Resurrection in John 20

Chapter 5

The Resurrection in John 21
—Missionary and Pastoral Directives for the Church

The Easter season stretches from Holy Saturday to Pentecost. The church thus enables us to realize that Jesus' emergence from the dead and from the tomb, his ascent to God, his glorification, and the gift of the Spirit are all one mystery. The evangelists, however, for narrative purposes and from the viewpoint of the human beings living in time who are involved in the story, have to describe as taking place on different occasions the various aspects of that one great resurrection mystery. John 20:1 portrays Jesus as already having risen when Mary Magdalene comes to the now empty tomb "early on the first day of the week, while it was still dark." When later in the day Jesus appears to Mary Magdalene, he says to her (20:17). "I am ascending to my Father and your Father, to my God and your God." On the evening of that same day when he appears to the disciples, he breathes on them and says (20:22), "Receive the Holy Spirit."[96] The gift of the Spirit is one of the church-founding aspects of the resurrection.

The presence in John of another chapter (21) involving an appearance of Jesus is also related to the issue of church-founding. Most critical scholars recognize that chapter 21, following upon the conclusion of the Gospel in 20:30-31, is an editorial (or redactional) addition to the Gospel. In fact, despite the editorial seams (21:1, 14) that facilitate the joining of John 20 and 21, the appearance of Jesus in John 21 seems

[96]Luke for his own structural purposes stretches out the description: ascension to heaven takes place either on Easter Sunday evening (Luke 24:51) or 40 days later (Acts 1:3, 9-10), and the gift of the Spirit takes place on Pentecost (50 days after Passover).

totally independent of the appearances in John 20; for the disciples act as if they had never seen Jesus before. While all that analysis of composition is important in the total exegetical picture, the interpretation of a Gospel in the liturgical context must work with the text *as it now stands.*[97] Accordingly I shall read the appearance in John 21 as granted to those who have seen the risen Lord and received the gift of the Spirit in John 20, just as the account reads in the Bible without critical presuppositions. Also I suggest that the appearance in John 21 can be understood more profoundly if one keeps in mind the context supplied by the whole Gospel,[98] and leaves aside the possibility that this may be an independently appended chapter.

Although all the events in chapter 21 take place in the one site on the one morning as a sequential series, the editorial remark in 21:14 offers justification for speaking of two parts, consisting of 21:1-14 and 21:15-24. The final verse (21:25) is a conclusion to the whole Gospel and does not apply specifically to the resurrection appearance. For convenience' sake we shall work with four subdivisions:

(1) 21:1-8:   The Appearance of Jesus at the Sea of Tiberias and the Miraculous Catch of Fish
(2) 21:9-14:   The Meal of Bread and Fish
(3) 21:15-19:   Jesus and Simon Peter
(4) 21:20-24:   Jesus and the Beloved Disciple

If one looks back to John 20, the same fascination with reactions to the risen Jesus by individuals (here: by the disciples, Simon Peter, the Beloved Disciple) is attested; but now the

---

[97]This approach is valid for more then liturgical purposes. No matter how likely our reconstruction of Fourth Gospel composition, the only known form of John has chapter 21 after 20. On the principle that such an order made sense to the one who produced it, we should comment on it.

[98]This approach was stressed above in the second paragraph of the Foreword.

The Resurrection in John 21

symbolism of action and message is more developed, as we shall see below.

The last time Jesus was in Galilee at this sea with his disciples was on the occasion of the multiplication of the loaves (John 6), and that event is implicitly recalled in this chapter. In John 6:67-70 Simon Peter took the initiative in speaking for the Twelve; here again he takes the initiative in proposing to go fishing, and arouses the others to go with him. Of the seven disciples listed, one reminds us of the beginning of the Gospel, for Nathaniel from Cana in Galilee (last mentioned in John 1:45-51) reappears here. Four more are members of the Twelve: Simon Peter, Thomas, and the sons of Zebedee. It is astonishing that these members of the Twelve who saw the risen Jesus in Jerusalem,[99] were sent out by him, and received the Holy Spirit as a grant of power over sin (20:21-23) are now simply fishing in Galilee. In particular, Thomas had a special encounter with the risen Jesus whom he confessed as Lord and God, but now gives no evidence of having been changed dramatically. John 21 has the effect of warning the readers that a move from belief in the risen Jesus to action based on that belief cannot be taken for granted. Disciples who came to believe in Jesus in John 20 are now engaged in ordinary activity without a sign of transformation.

In any case the disciples are unsuccessful in their fishing, for they catch nothing all night (21:3). Then at dawn Jesus is suddenly present on the shore—a description with a hint of mysteriousness. Though they have seen the risen Jesus twice

[99]The scene in John 20:19-23 presumably involved members of the the Twelve (footnote 87 above).

The Resurrection in John 21

before and though Thomas was invited to probe physically Jesus' hands and side, the disciples do not recognize him.[100] This failure to recognize, since it shows limitation on the part of those who *saw* the risen Jesus, may underline the beatitude uttered by Jesus to Thomas in 20:29: "Blessed are those who have *not* seen and yet have believed."

Thus far in John there has been recounted no scene where men fishing by the lake were called by Jesus to be his disciples and made "fishers of men." That scene was placed at the beginning of the Gospel by Mark (1:16-20; Matt 4:18-22) as the first major initiative of Jesus' ministry. Luke 5:1-11 has combined with that account a story of how, although Simon and the others had fished all night and caught nothing, they let down their nets at Jesus' instruction and caught so many fish that their nets were breaking. In other words, besides the common Synoptic symbolism whereby the disciples are made fishers of people, Luke's miraculous catch stresses that the mission guided by Jesus will be extraordinarily abundant. Placed at the beginning of the Gospel, this Synoptic treatment is predictive of a future that will come only when the public ministry of Jesus is over. John offers his form of the miraculous-catch story[101] after the resurrection with a much more immediate focus. The disciples were sent out by the risen Jesus in 20:21; yet they have resumed the fishing trade. Jesus now uses that trade to symbolize what they must begin

[100]This non-recognition that we have encountered in several resurrection appearances also served apologetically: it militated against the thesis that the disciples were credulous and looking for the resurrection so that they might have identified another person as Jesus.

[101]Many scholars think that the miraculous-catch story has a more original locus in Luke, i.e., that it was a ministry story which John has placed after the resurrection. The fact that Luke adds it to a Marcan context suggests to me that it was a free-floating story without a fixed locus and that Luke has inserted it where he thought best. Whether John's postresurrectional context is more original depends on whether the appearance of Jesus to Peter was integrally connected to it, rather than joined to it by John.

The Resurrection in John 21

to do. As in Luke, Jesus' assistance reverses human incapability to make a catch: so many are the fish caught in John 21 that the disciples cannot haul in the net.

The miraculous catch brings about recognition of the risen Jesus in a pattern that has some similarity to the recognition process in John 20. In that previous chapter we saw a sequence of reactions: the Beloved Disciple believed first, simply on the evidence of the garments in the tomb (20:8). So also here he is the first to recognize the Lord, simply on the evidence of the catch (21:7). In John 20, although she did not recognize Jesus at first, Mary Magdalene was the next person to know him when she heard him call her by name and seemingly she went to clutch him (20:16-17). Here, through the Beloved Disciple as intermediary,[102] Simon Peter hears that it is the Lord and immediately jumps into the sea to go to Jesus on the land. No interpreter is certain what John means precisely when he writes in 21:7 of Simon Peter adjusting garments over his nakedness before he springs into the sea. Besides the more obvious meaning that he donned a garment when he previously had nothing on, his action could mean that he belted or tucked in the only garment he had on over his naked body. Perhaps the purpose of the description is to have Peter show respect before Jesus. In any case the Johannine scene portrays Peter's spontaneity and love of the Lord—a motif Jesus will pick up later in the dialogue with Peter (21:15-17).

EPISODE IN 21:9-14: THE MEAL OF BREAD AND FISH
Although this episode introduces a new topic centered on a meal, what happens is intrinsically linked to the catch of fish and will fill out the missionary symbolism of that catch. In 20:20 the disciples came to experience the reality of the risen Lord only after the Beloved Disciple and Mary Magdalene. So also here the disciples, not knowing that it is Jesus, have

---

[102]See also John 13:23-26; 18:15-16.

The Resurrection in John 21

carried on the fishing chore of dragging the net full of fish toward the shore. When they arrive, they see a charcoal fire already burning, with fish and bread on it. Jesus, to them still a stranger, asks for fish from the fresh catch; and Simon Peter, knowing that this is a command of *the Lord*, hastens to drag the net ashore. The symbolism of the catch is now forcefully emphasized by enumerating 153 large fish; yet, we are told, the net is not broken. Scholars have exercised great ingenuity in explaining the number. It may simply be a touch to underline the eyewitness quality of the scene (see 21:24); it may represent the total number of different species of fish known to Greek zoologists (as suggested by Jerome: in that case its function is to symbolize the universality of the mission); or it may be a play on the numerical value of the names in Ezek 47:10 where fishermen stand on the shore of the Dead Sea from *Engedi* to *Eneglaim,* spreading their nets, and there are as many fish in the Sea enriched by the stream from the Temple as there are in the Mediterranean (in which case John is showing the fulfillment of OT eschatological prophecy). What is certain is that the number and size of the fish show how successful the disciples can be with Jesus' help. One is reminded of John 4:37-38 where Jesus sends disciples to reap an abundant harvest that they did not sow. The symbolism of the net that has not been torn has also been the subject of scholarly discussion. In John 17:19-20 Jesus prays for the oneness of those who believe in him through the word of those whom he sends out, and so the untorn net may symbolize the unity of those "caught" by the disciples whom the risen Jesus has sent out (20:21).[103]

[103]Other passages dealing with unity include John 10:16 where the "Good Shepherd" says that he has other sheep not of this fold, and that he has to bring them so that there will be one sheep herd, one shepherd. This passage is relevant for chapter 21 because in 21:15-17 Jesus uses the image of shepherding once more. A possible parallel for the net that was not torn may be the tunic of Jesus that was not torn or divided (19:23-24), which many see as a symbol of unity.

The Resurrection in John 21

Granted all these reported details of the catch, it is truly astounding that the disciples have not recognized the Lord. John 21:12 (somewhat hesitantly) at last attributes knowledge to them as Jesus invites them, "Come and eat your breakfast." (Is it by chance that these last words spoken by Jesus to the disciples in John are an invitation even as were the first words spoken by Jesus to them in 1:39: "Come and see"?[104]) Other recounted appearances of the risen Jesus are associated with meals: Luke 24:30, 42; perhaps Acts 1:4; Acts 10:41; Mark 16:14. Luke (p. 50 above) stressed a eucharistic aspect in the meal of the risen Jesus with the two disciples at Emmaus (24:30-35: they knew him in the breaking of the bread). John 21:12-13 seems to fit into that ambiance. The disciples know Jesus as the Lord in the context of a meal; and we are told that Jesus came and took bread and gave it to them, and similarly the fish. The last time he was at this lake Jesus took the loaves; and when he had given thanks (*eucharistein*), he distributed it to those seated, and likewise the fish (John 6:11). That scene of the multiplication of the loaves was interpreted eucharistically in John 6:51b-58: "The bread that I shall give for the life of the world is my flesh. . . . If you do not eat the flesh of the Son of Man and drink his blood, you have no life in you." Thus there is reason to think that the readers of John might well reflect on their own eucharists as they read how the risen Jesus fed the disciples at the lake and might be challenged to recognize that it is the risen Lord who is present in those eucharists.

EPISODE IN 21:15-19: JESUS AND SIMON PETER

Tradition (Luke 24:34; 1 Cor 15:5) has it that, among those who would be apostolic preachers of the resurrection, Simon, called Cephas or Peter, was the first to see the risen Jesus. That appearance to Simon is nowhere recounted in the

[104]Notice, however, that there are different Greek words for "Come" in the two passages.

Gospels; yet hidden beneath the surface of John 21 the story may still be present in terms of an appearance in Galilee to Peter when he was fishing. This appearance may have included the questioning of Peter by Jesus and a commissioning of him to support or care for others.[105] What is fascinating in the sequence of chapter 21 is the shift of topic. Peter was part of the group of disciples who made the huge catch of fish; thus he was part of the general apostolic mission that would bring in large numbers of believers. But now Jesus speaks to him alone *about sheep!* The catching of fish is an apt image for an evangelizing mission; but to picture the ongoing care of those brought in by that mission one has to change the image. We call this care of those already converted ''pastoral,'' precisely because of the set use of flock and sheep in this connection. Thus the readers of John 21 are invited to see in Peter the combination of missionary and pastor.[106]

If we are familiar with Johannine language, several factors in the dialogue of 21:15-17 stand out. Jesus addresses Peter as ''Simon, son of John.'' The only other time Jesus addressed him thus was in 1:42 when Jesus gave him the name ''Cephas (which means Peter).'' In other words in John this is an address that leads to an identification, either by name (as in 1:42) or by role (here). The role of shepherding the

---

[105]Some would relate to John 21:15-17 other sayings of Jesus to Peter now scattered through the Gospels. Matt 16:16-18, where Peter is made the rock on which the church will be built, is often thought to have had originally a postresurrectional context. A related saying in Luke 22:31-32, where Jesus prays for Simon that his faith will not fail and that when he has turned he will strengthen his brothers, is difficult to fit into a postresurrectional context.

[106]In the genuine Pauline letters Paul emerges as a missionary; but in the postPauline Pastorals (1-2 Timothy, Titus) we see Paul wrestling with permanent church structure. Thus a movement from missionary to pastor is attested in the remembrance of Paul as well as of Peter.

The Resurrection in John 21

sheep, like the name Peter, signifies this man's special identity in the Christian community.

Before this role is assigned, Peter is asked three times: "Do you love me?";[107] or more precisely, the first time Jesus asks, "Do you love me more than these?" If "these" refers to the other disciples who did not recognize Jesus in the meal (and who now seem almost to have disappeared from the scene), then we are reminded of Simon Peter's boastful reaction in 13:37 at the Last Supper. There, after Jesus warned of the impossibility of following him to the cross, Peter objected, "Lord, why can't I follow you now? I will lay down my life for you." Against that background Peter might now have claimed to love the risen Jesus more than the others, for there is no greater love than the willingness to lay down one's life for one's friend (15:13). Moreover, in the present chapter, Peter hastened to Jesus from the boat while the other disciples did not recognize him and stayed in the boat. Does Peter still think of himself as the most loving? From his response it is now apparent that Peter has been chastened by the failure he manifested in denying Jesus; for he does not compare his love with that of the other disciples[108] but confines himself to a simple, personal affirmation of love. Even in that affirmation Peter trusts himself to Jesus' knowledge. Previously, when Simon Peter boasted about his willingness

[107]The verb is alternated thus: in Jesus' three questions: *agapan, agapan, philein*; in Peter's response: *philein, philein, philein*. Similarly there is alternation in the verbs that govern the sheep ("to feed, pasture": *boskein, poimainein, boskein*), and in the noun for sheep (*arnion, probaton, probation*). Older commentators, overly influenced by classical Greek, sought precise shades of meaning in these choices; rather they are simply stylistic variations.

[108]Most scholars understand "more than these" personally, i.e., "more than these disciples do"; but another possible understanding is to take "these" as a neuter accusative: "Do you love me more than you love these things [i.e., your ordinary pursuits like fishing]." Then, Jesus would be asking Peter to leave his ordinary life and devote himself to serving the followers of Jesus.

The Resurrection in John 21

to follow Jesus even unto death, Jesus showed that he knew Peter better than Peter knew himself by predicting three denials before cockcrow. Now, although Simon Peter believes with all his heart that he loves Jesus in total fidelity, all that he is willing to claim is: "You know that I love you."

There is no doubt, then, that the threefold pattern and some of the context of the questions and answers in 21:15-17 are set over against the pattern of the threefold denial of Jesus by Peter in the high priest's court (18:15-18, 25-27). It is noteworthy that in the three Synoptic Gospels, when the cock crowed, we were told that Peter recalled Jesus' predictions of three denials before cockcrow (Mark 14:72; Matt 26:75; Luke 22:61); but that was not said in John. Perhaps we are meant to think that only here after the resurrection Peter is reminded of Jesus' prediction by being questioned three times.

Yet the dialogue between the risen Jesus and Simon Peter has a more immediate purpose than Peter's repentance. A major pastoral role is being assigned to him—indeed a role that in Johannine theology is highly unexpected. Those scholars who have worked with the Johannine Epistles and have sought to read between the lines of the Fourth Gospel in order to reconstruct the life of the Johannine community[109] have noticed the lack of titles customarily used for New Testament church authorities. In 1 Cor 12:28 Paul states, "God has appointed in the church first apostles, second prophets, third teachers"; yet the whole Johannine corpus calls none apostles, mentions among Christians only those prophets who are false (1 Jn 4:1), and states that the readers have no need of anyone to teach them (1 John 2:27). 3 John 9 shows a dislike for a man named Diotrephes who likes to put himself first (in authority) in a local church. To this depreciation of human authorities one must add the evidence

[109]See, for instance, R. E. Brown, *The Community of the Beloved Disciple* (New York: Paulist, 1979) and the bibliography cited therein.

The Resurrection in John 21

of John 10. In the 80s the image of shepherding a flock was in use in several New Testament areas as a symbol for the work of the presbyter-bishops.[110] Yet in John 10 Jesus identifies *himself* as the model shepherd, the sole gate by which one should enter the sheepfold, so that anyone who does not enter by that gate is a thief and a robber (10:1, 7). Is the assignment of a shepherding role to Simon Peter symbolic of a change in Johannine attitude? By tradition Simon Peter was regarded as the first of the Twelve and the granting of authority to him by Jesus at the end of John (indeed, in an appended chapter) could suggest the latterly realization by the Johannine community that without human shepherds the community would split up (along the lines attested in 1 John 2:19).

In any case, if John 21:15-17 is a modification of the sole shepherd role assigned to Jesus in John 10, careful qualifications are incorporated in John 21 to make certain that Johannine values are preserved. No pastoral assignment is made without the assurance that Simon Peter loves Jesus. The model disciple of this community is the one whom Jesus loves. The Paraclete/Spirit is promised to those who love Jesus and keep his commands (14:15). Thus the mutual love that exists between Jesus and the believers is a most important factor in this community's life, and that criterion is applied to anyone who would exercise pastoral care. Ours is a time when people quarrel over who should have authority in the church with the "have-nots" polarized against the "haves." The argument is advanced that to hold pastoral office is a human right or at least the right of all who are baptized. John's primary concern is of quite a different sort. The one who would care for the sheep must first show love for Jesus, even to the point of laying down life itself for him (as we shall see below). That criterion is a challenge both to the "haves" and the "have-nots."

[110]Acts 20:17, 28; 1 Pet 5:1-4; see also Eph 4:11 (apostles, prophets, evangelists, *pastors*, teachers).

The Resurrection in John 21

Another qualification is imposed by the dialogue of John 21:15-17. Even though Peter is charged with caring for the sheep, Jesus continues to speak of those as "my lambs, my sheep." The flock never passes into the proprietorship of the human shepherd; no one can ever take the place of Jesus. Speaking of himself as the model shepherd, Jesus claimed, "I know mine, and mine know me" (10:14). His was a voice that the sheep would recognize as he called them by name (10:3, 5, 16). The priority of a personal relationship to Jesus on the part of those who constitute the flock is not neglected now that a human structure of authority is being established. Only Jesus can use the word "mine," even though Peter feeds the sheep. Inevitably in the course of decades and centuries the church would take on coloring and values from a secular society where visible authority is most important and where such authority tends to be possessive. The language of the Johannine Jesus serves as a leavening corrective against all tendencies, however well-intentioned, of those in authority to speak of "my people, my parishioners."

What Peter is told to do is to feed or care for the sheep. Because the king in Old Testament imagery was described as a shepherd, the task of pasturing the flock was often understood to involve ruling.[111] Yet the notion of ruling authority has at most a minor place in Jesus' commission to Simon Peter. In chapter 10, which describes the role of the good or model shepherd, Jesus never talks about ruling. The role of the shepherd is to lead the sheep out to pasture, to know them personally so that they feel close to him, and especially to lay down his life for the sheep (10:11, 15). At the Last Supper Peter boasted that he would be willing to lay down his life for Jesus (13:37-38), but he failed miserably when challenged to do so. Evidently Jesus has not forgotten that preamble to Peter's denials, and so in the context of commis-

---

[111]This is illustrated by the use of *poimainein* (footnote 107 above) in the Septuagint of 2 Sam 5:2; 1 Chron 17:6.

The Resurrection in John 21

sioning him to feed the sheep Jesus now warns Peter about death (21:18-19). If Peter is given care of the sheep, he will be required to lay down his life. The description of Peter's stretching out his hands, being fastened with a belt, and being led forcibly to where he would not go is surely a reference to a penal death (21:19: "The kind of death by which Peter was to glorify God"). Perhaps more specifically it is a reference to Peter's crucifixion. In either case, the likely date at which this is being written is after Peter had glorified God as a martyr, so that John knows that Peter's following Jesus to death—an aborted action on Good Friday—was eventually verified on Vatican Hill. The Simon Peter of John 21 who three times states, "Lord, you know that I love you," keeps his word by laying down his life for the one whom he loves, as an essential part of the care of the sheep assigned to him. In that action he obeyed the last words ever spoken to him by Jesus: "Follow me" (21:19b, 22). Such behavior was far more important in the Johannine estimation of Peter as shepherding than the issue of how much power Peter had over the sheep.

EPISODE IN 21:20-24:
JESUS AND THE BELOVED DISCIPLE
Despite the dialogue just discussed and the unique pastoral role given to Peter, he is not the most important follower of Jesus in Johannine thought. The disciple whom Jesus loved was mentioned early in the scene as the first to recognize Jesus and the one to inform Peter. We now discover that this disciple is still present. Indeed it is interesting that this disciple was left without an introduction when first named (21:7) but is now introduced as the figure who had lain on Jesus' breast at the Last Supper (21:20). The scene with Simon Peter reminded us of the boasts made by him at the Last Supper and his subsequent threefold denial of Jesus; a more intimate relationship to Jesus is recalled for the Beloved Disciple.

The Resurrection in John 21

The readers would almost have forgotten the presence of this disciple; now suddenly he is mentioned as following Jesus and Peter, but seemingly standing behind. Is that positioning a way of hinting that in the estimation of the larger church it is Peter the shepherd who would stand in front? Peter himself raises the question, "What about this man?" Curiously this disciple to whom no pastoral authority over the flock has been assigned is a subject of concern to the human figure who has just received authority. Is this because the Beloved Disciple really does not fit easily into a value system established by authority? In these last verses of the Gospel we find peculiarly Johannine values exemplified in a striking way. To be a disciple whom Jesus loves is in the end more important than to be assigned church authority! If Peter has a primacy of pastoral care, this disciple has another primacy bestowed by Jesus' love.

Peter is to die a martyr's death, but Jesus has a destiny for this disciple that is less dramatic but more enduring. The play on the disciple's remaining until Jesus comes is a final literary touch in a Gospel that has played with double-meaning terms throughout as a way of showing how human beings misunderstand, because they think on the level of this world which is below while God's world is above. Even some of the Johannine community ("the brothers" of 21:23) have misunderstood this final play on words. They thought that when Jesus said, "Suppose I would like him to remain until I come," he meant that the disciple would not die. But John 21:23 tells us with absolute assurance that Jesus did not mean that—an assurance that probably indicates that the disciple was already dead. Why then did Jesus even raise the issue of the disciple's remaining? A modern biblical critic may use this passage to discuss Jesus' knowledge of the time of the second coming and may point to Mark 13:32 which says that even the Son does not know of that day or that hour.[112] Yet while limitations in Jesus' earthly knowledge

The Resurrection in John 21

may well explain the historical origin of the saying in John 21, this Gospel where Jesus is virtually omniscient can scarcely be interpreted as implying a limitation on Jesus' part. Does the Johannine answer as to why Jesus made the statement[113] lie in the dual nature of the Beloved Disciple? John 21:24 clearly presents him as a historical person who gave witness; as such he died and did not remain until Jesus comes. At most he remains on in his witness and in the written tradition preserved in the Fourth Gospel. Yet in another sense the Beloved Disciple represents the perfect disciple— the *kind* of disciple that Jesus loves. If Peter embodies church authority, this disciple embodies all those who, although they may not be commissioned to care for the sheep, are deeply loved by Jesus because they love him and keep his commandments. In that sense, the kind of disciple whom Jesus loves will remain until Jesus comes. If the last words of Jesus in Matthew (28:20) are that he will be with us to the end of time, the last words of Jesus in John may be affirming the final fruit of the resurrection: a believing community of Christians will remain until Jesus returns.

[112]See also Mark 9:1: Some of Jesus' contemporaries will not taste death before they see the kingdom of God come in power.

[113]Some speculation about Johannine thought is justified here because, although John rejects a misunderstanding, he does not explain in what sense the saying conveys truth.

The Resurrection in John 21

Works of Raymond E. Brown published by The Liturgical Press:

The Gospel and Epistles of John—A Concise Commentary
Recent Discoveries and the Biblical World (A Michael Glazier Book)
A Coming Christ in Advent (Matthew 1 and Luke 1)
An Adult Christ at Christmas (Matthew 2 and Luke 2)
A Crucified Christ in Holy Week (Passion Narratives)
A Risen Christ in Eastertime (Resurrection Narratives)